P9-DNP-230

❧❦❧

FOR:

Bev Colisino

May the Lord of peace himself give you peace
at all times and in every way.

2 THESSALONIANS 3:16

FROM:

_____

❧❦❧

Requests for information should be addressed to:
    Inspirio, the Gift Group of Zondervan
    Grand Rapids, Michigan 49530

Senior Editor: Gwen Ellis
Project Editor: Sarah Hupp
Designer: Chris Gannon
Production Editor: Molly Detweiler

Printed in China

01 02 03/HK/ 5 4

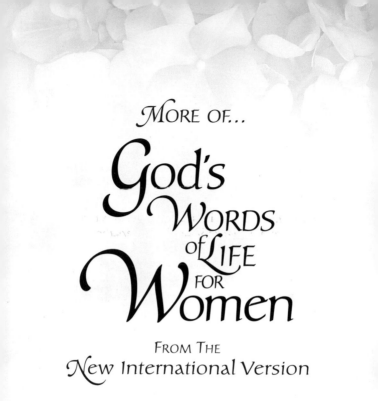

MORE OF...

God's WORDS of LIFE for Women

FROM THE
New International Version

inspirio
The gift group of Zondervan

GOD'S WORDS
OF LIFE ON

Do to others as you would have them do to you.

LUKE 6:31

Jesus said, "He who receives you receives me, and he who receives me receives the one who sent me."

MATTHEW 10:40

Jesus said, "I have set you an example that you should do as I have done for you."

JOHN 13:15

How good and pleasant it is when brothers live together in unity!

PSALM 133:1

Jesus said, "You have heard that it was said, 'Love your neighbor and hate your enemy.' But I tell you: Love your enemies and pray for those who persecute you."

MATTHEW 5:43-44

To love God with all your heart, with all your understanding and with all your strength, and to love your neighbor as yourself is more important than all burnt offerings and sacrifices.

MARK 12:33

GOD'S WORDS OF LIFE ON
ACCEPTANCE

Jesus said, "I tell you the truth, anyone who gives you a cup of water in my name because you belong to Christ will certainly not lose his reward."

MARK 9:41

Jesus said, "My command is this: Love each other as I have loved you. Greater love has no one than this, that he lay down his life for his friends."

JOHN 15:12-13

Be devoted to one another in brotherly love. Honor one another above yourselves.

ROMANS 12:10

May the Lord make your love increase and over-flow for each other and for everyone else, just as ours does for you.

1 THESSALONIANS 3:12

Let us consider how we may spur one another on toward love and good deeds.

HEBREWS 10:24

If you really keep the royal law found in Scripture, "Love your neighbor as yourself," you are doing right.

JAMES 2:8

ACCEPTANCE

Above all, love each other deeply, because love covers over a multitude of sins.

1 PETER 4:8

Whoever hates his brother is in the darkness and walks around in the darkness; he does not know where he is going, because the darkness has blinded him.

1 JOHN 2:11

God has shown me that I should not call any man impure or unclean.

ACTS 10:28

Dear friends, let us love one another, for love comes from God. Everyone who loves has been born of God and knows God.

1 JOHN 4:7

OVERLOOKING OUR DIFFERENCES

Rain, sleet or snow, Bill was always barefoot. While he was attending college he had become a Christian. At this time a well-dressed, middle-class church across the street from the campus wanted to develop more of a ministry to the students.

One day Bill decided to worship there. He walked into this church, wearing his blue jeans, tee shirt and of course no shoes. People looked a bit uncomfortable, but no one said anything. So Bill began walking down the aisle looking for a seat. The church was quite crowded that Sunday, so as he got down to the front pew and realized that there were no seats, he just squatted on the carpet.

Suddenly an elderly man began walking down the aisle toward the boy. The church became utterly silent; all eyes were focused on him. When the man reached Bill, with some difficulty he lowered himself and sat down next to him on the carpet. He and Bill worshiped together on the floor that Sunday.

Grace is always that way. It gives without the receiver realizing how great the gift really is. As this man loved his brother, so must we.

REBECCA MANLEY PIPPERT

"Even to your old age and gray hairs I am he, I am he who will sustain you. I have made you and I will carry you; I will sustain you and I will rescue you," says the Lord.

ISAIAH 46:4

May the Lord bless you from Zion all the days of your life; may you see the prosperity of Jerusalem, and may you live to see your children's children.

PSALM 128:5-6

Is not wisdom found among the aged? Does not long life bring understanding?

JOB 12:12

Your children will be many, and your descendants like the grass of the earth. You will come to the grave in full vigor, like sheaves gathered in season.

JOB 5:25-26

Children's children are a crown to the aged, and parents are the pride of their children.

PROVERBS 17:6

Honor your father and your mother, so that you may live long in the land the LORD your God is giving you.

EXODUS 20:12

Even when I am old and gray, do not forsake me,
O God, till I declare your power to the next generation, your might to all who are to come.

PSALM 71:18

Teach us to number our days aright, that we may
gain a heart of wisdom.

PSALM 90:12

Gray hair is a crown of splendor; it is attained by
a righteous life.

PROVERBS 16:31

They will still bear fruit in old age, they will stay
fresh and green, proclaiming, "The LORD is
upright; he is my Rock, and there is no wickedness in him."

PSALM 92:14-15

"With long life will I satisfy him and show him my
salvation," says the LORD.

PSALM 91:16

He has made everything beautiful in its time. He
has also set eternity in the hearts of men; yet
they cannot fathom what God has done from
beginning to end.

ECCLESIASTES 3:11

AGING

He asked you for life, and you gave it to him—
length of days, for ever and ever.

PSALM 21:4

The fear of the LORD adds length to life, but the
years of the wicked are cut short.

PROVERBS 10:27

"Keep my commands in your heart, for they will
prolong your life many years and bring you prosperity," says the LORD.

PROVERBS 3:1-2

The glory of young men is their strength, gray hair
the splendor of the old.

PROVERBS 20:29

Long life to you! Good health to you and your
household! And good health to all that is yours!

1 SAMUEL 25:6

THE PILGRIM ROAD

Let's be honest. Old age entails suffering. I'm acutely aware of this now as I watch my mother, once so alive and alert and quick, now so quiet and confused and slow. We see the preview of "coming attractions," ourselves in her shoes, and ponder what this interval means in terms of the glory of God in an old woman.

It would be terrifying if it weren't for something that ought to make the Christian's attitude toward aging utterly distinct from the rest. We know it's not for nothing (see Ephesians 1:9-10).

In the meantime, we look at what's happening—limitations of hearing, seeing, moving, digesting, remembering; distortions of countenance, figure and perspective. If that's all we could see, we'd certainly want a face-lift or something.

But we're on a pilgrim road. It's rough and steep, and it winds uphill to the very end. We can lift up our eyes and see the unseen: a celestial city, a light, a welcome and an ineffable face. We shall behold him. We shall be like him. And that makes a difference in how we go about aging.

ELISABETH ELLIOT

Charm is deceptive, and beauty is fleeting, but a woman who fears the LORD is to be praised.

PROVERBS 31:30

How beautiful on the mountains are the feet of those who bring good news, who proclaim peace, who bring good tidings, who proclaim salvation, who say to Zion, "Your God reigns!"

ISAIAH 52:7

Your beauty should not come from outward adornment, such as braided hair and the wearing of gold jewelry and fine clothes. Instead, it should be that of your inner self, the unfading beauty of a gentle and quiet spirit, which is of great worth in God's sight. For this is the way the holy women of the past who put their hope in God used to make themselves beautiful.

1 PETER 3:3-5

I praise you because I am fearfully and wonderfully made; your works are wonderful, I know that full well.

PSALM 139:14

God has made everything beautiful in its time.

ECCLESIASTES 3:11

BEAUTY

"Your fame spread among the nations on account of your beauty, because the splendor I had given you made your beauty perfect," declares the Sovereign Lᴏʀᴅ.

Eᴢᴇᴋɪᴇʟ 16:14

This is what I seek: that I may dwell in the house of the Lᴏʀᴅ all the days of my life, to gaze upon the beauty of the Lᴏʀᴅ and to seek him in his temple.

Pѕᴀʟᴍ 27:4

A wife of noble character who can find? She is worth far more than rubies . . . She is clothed with strength and dignity; she can laugh at the days to come. She speaks with wisdom, and faithful instruction is on her tongue.

Pʀᴏᴠᴇʀʙѕ 31:10,25-26

The Lᴏʀᴅ does not look at the things man looks at. Man looks at the outward appearance, but the Lᴏʀᴅ looks at the heart.

1 Sᴀᴍᴜᴇʟ 16:7

How beautiful you are, my darling!
   Oh, how beautiful!
   Your eyes are doves.

Sᴏɴɢ ᴏꜰ Sᴏɴɢѕ 1:15

BEAUTY

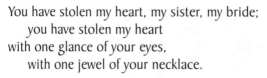

You have stolen my heart, my sister, my bride;
   you have stolen my heart
with one glance of your eyes,
   with one jewel of your necklace.

SONG OF SONGS 4:9

The LORD their God will save them on that day
   as the flock of his people.
They will sparkle in his land
   like jewels in a crown.
How attractive and beautiful they will be!
   Grain will make the young men thrive,
   and new wine the young women.

ZECHARIAH 9:16–17

THE YOU INSIDE

Last night we went to the business meeting at church, and it began to rain. By the time we got there, all the good parking places were taken and we had to walk quite a way. I had on my best white slacks too. It would be understandable to get a few little mud spots on the bottoms, but when we entered the brightly lit room I discovered I had a big muddy smear on my stomach.

"Let it dry," my husband advised. "Then you can brush it off."

I had to give my report before it dried. I knew everyone was looking at the mud, so I kept trying to hold pages over it, and I dropped some. When I bent down to pick them up, I bumped heads with the moderator who had bent down to help me.

"Does my girl feel grumpy?" my husband asked at breakfast the next day.

I groaned. "How can you love anybody who is so sloppy—so overweight—so klutzy?" I stormed. When I began to cry he hugged me.

"If I was all rolled up in bandages," he said, "and you couldn't see me, would you still love me?"

"Of course," I snapped. "It would still be you inside."

"Guess that answers your question." He kissed me. "I love the you inside."

MAB GRAFF HOOVER

17

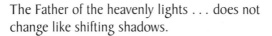

The Father of the heavenly lights . . . does not change like shifting shadows.

JAMES 1:17

I the LORD do not change.

MALACHI 3:6

Jesus Christ is the same yesterday and today and forever.

HEBREWS 13:8

If anyone is in Christ, he is a new creation; the old has gone, the new has come!

2 CORINTHIANS 5:17

I will put my laws in their minds and write them on their hearts. I will be their God, and they will be my people. No longer will a man teach his neighbor, or a man his brother, saying, "Know the Lord," because they will all know me, from the least of them to the greatest. For I will forgive their wickedness and will remember their sins no more.

HEBREWS 8:10–12

He who is the Glory of Israel does not lie or change his mind; for he is not a man, that he should change his mind.

1 SAMUEL 15:29

Set your hearts on things above, where Christ is seated at the right hand of God. Set your minds on things above, not on earthly things. For you died, and your life is now hidden with Christ in God.

Colossians 3:1–3

You, however, are controlled not by the sinful nature but by the Spirit, if the Spirit of God lives in you.

Romans 8:9

You were taught, with regard to your former way of life, to put off your old self, which is being corrupted by its deceitful desires; to be made new in the attitude of your minds; and to put on the new self, created to be like God in true righteousness and holiness.

Ephesians 4:22–24

See, I am doing a new thing! Now it springs up; do you not perceive it? I am making a way in the desert and streams in the wasteland.

Isaiah 43:19

Our old self was crucified with him so that the body of sin might be done away with, that we should no longer be slaves to sin—because anyone who has died has been freed from sin.

Romans 6:6–7

Behold, I will create new heavens and a new earth. The former things will not be remembered, nor will they come to mind. But be glad and rejoice forever in what I will create, for I will create Jerusalem to be a delight and its people a joy.

ISAIAH 65:17–18

By dying to what once bound us, we have been released from the law so that we serve in the new way of the Spirit, and not in the old way of the written code.

ROMANS 7:6

Then I saw a new heaven and a new earth, for the first heaven and the first earth had passed away, and there was no longer any sea. I saw the Holy City, the new Jerusalem, coming down out of heaven from God, prepared as a bride beautifully dressed for her husband. And I heard a loud voice from the throne saying, "Now the dwelling of God is with men, and he will live with them. They will be his people, and God himself will be with them and be their God. He will wipe every tear from their eyes. There will be no more death or mourning or crying or pain, for the old order of things has passed away." He who was seated on the throne said, "I am making everything new!" Then he said, "Write this down, for these words are trustworthy and true."

REVELATION 21:1–5

TRUST THE GOD OF CHANGE

Life for most of us is not a steady-paced stroll through time, with a beginning, a middle, and an end, like a well-constructed play. It's filled with change. We change schools, careers, homes, relationships, and "images" almost as casually as our great-grandparents changed horses.

Not that all change is by choice. A marriage dissolves. Cherished friendships change in character or another person's choice cuts directly across our own, bringing us where we never wanted to be. A career change, voluntary or involuntary, may disrupt our lives. Financial losses sweep away our props. Even geographic change can be disorienting.

For the believer, then, the question is vital: Is our God the Lord of change? Will he be with us in change, especially when it strains our trust to its limit? Ironically, while we trust him with our eternal fate, we may find it difficult to trust him for next month's car payment, a new relationship, or an unexpected turn in our lives.

In the kaleidoscopic whirl of our life patterns, it can be enormously reassuring to remind ourselves that God is unchanging: "I the LORD do not change" (Malachi 3:6).

GINI ANDREWS

I have learned to be content whatever the circumstances. I know what it is to be in need, and I know what it is to have plenty. I have learned the secret of being content in any and every situation, whether well fed or hungry, whether living in plenty or in want.

PHILIPPIANS 4:11–12

Godliness with contentment is great gain. For we brought nothing into the world, and we can take nothing out of it. But if we have food and clothing, we will be content with that.

1 TIMOTHY 6:6–8

Keep your lives free from the love of money and be content with what you have, because God has said, "Never will I leave you; never will I forsake you." So we say with confidence, "The LORD is my helper; I will not be afraid. What can man do to me?"

HEBREWS 13:5–6

The boundary lines have fallen for me in pleasant places; surely I have a delightful inheritance.

PSALM 16:6

A cheerful look brings joy to the heart, and good news gives health to the bones.

PROVERBS 15:30

Be still before the LORD and wait patiently for him; do not fret when men succeed in their ways, when they carry out their wicked schemes. Refrain from anger and turn from wrath; do not fret—it leads only to evil. For evil men will be cut off, but those who hope in the LORD will inherit the land.

PSALM 37:7–9

Better the little that the righteous have than the wealth of many wicked; for the power of the wicked will be broken, but the LORD upholds the righteous.

PSALM 37:16–17

A happy heart makes the face cheerful.

PROVERBS 15:13

Better a little with the fear of the LORD than great wealth with turmoil. Better a meal of vegetables where there is love than a fattened calf with hatred.

PROVERBS 15:16–17

Better a little with righteousness than much gain with injustice.

PROVERBS 16:8

Better a dry crust with peace and quiet than a house full of feasting, with strife.

PROVERBS 17:1

Keep falsehood and lies far from me; give me neither poverty nor riches, but give me only my daily bread.

PROVERBS 30:8

That everyone may eat and drink, and find satisfaction in all his toil—this is the gift of God.

ECCLESIASTES 3:13

Better one handful with tranquillity than two handfuls with toil and chasing after the wind.

ECCLESIASTES 4:6

Go, eat your food with gladness, and drink your wine with a joyful heart, for it is now that God favors what you do. Always be clothed in white, and always anoint your head with oil.

ECCLESIASTES 9:7–8

Each one should retain the place in life that the Lord assigned to him and to which God has called him.

1 CORINTHIANS 7:17

&❧

A SIMPLE LIFE OF CONTENTMENT

Ecclesiastes has been described as a book about "rhythms and ruts." But Ecclesiastes also offers hope for breaking out of the rut. In 4:5 the poem alludes to the delicate balance between work and rest. It says that he who lacks ambition and a work ethic "ruins himself." On the other hand, the problem with "two handfuls" is that it leads to "chasing after the wind" (4:6). The person who is motivated by envy will never have enough.

A happy balance is achieved when one holds "one handful with tranquillity" (4:6). If we live with a spirit of contentment and gratitude, we have an empty hand to lift in praise, to extend to a needy neighbor, or to help lift up a friend (4:10).

Less is best when it is accompanied by "quiet." In I Thessalonians 4:11-12 Paul describes this lifestyle: "Make it your ambition to lead a quiet life, to mind your own business and to work with your hands, just as we told you, so that your daily life may win the respect of outsiders."

"Dear Lord, help me to lead a simple life. May I not slip into futility and the chaos of overabundance. Amen."

REVEREND DR. DELORES CARPENTER

This I call to mind and therefore I have hope: Because of the LORD's great love we are not consumed, for his compassions never fail. They are new every morning; great is your faithfulness.

LAMENTATIONS 3:21–23

Act with courage, and may the LORD be with those who do well.

2 CHRONICLES 19:11

Because the hand of the LORD my God was on me, I took courage.

EZRA 7:28

I eagerly expect and hope that I will in no way be ashamed, but will have sufficient courage so that now as always Christ will be exalted in my body, whether by life or by death.

PHILIPPIANS 1:20

Christ is faithful as a son over God's house. And we are his house, if we hold on to our courage and the hope of which we boast.

HEBREWS 3:6

The LORD himself goes before you and will be with you; he will never leave you nor forsake you. Do not be afraid; do not be discouraged."

DEUTERONOMY 31:8

Have I not commanded you? Be strong and courageous. Do not be terrified; do not be discouraged, for the LORD your God will be with you
wherever you go.

JOSHUA 1:9

You, O Lord, are a compassionate and gracious God,
slow to anger, abounding in love and faithfulness.

PSALM 86:15

Be strong and courageous, and do the work. Do
not be afraid or discouraged, for the LORD God,
my God, is with you. He will not fail you or forsake you.

1 CHRONICLES 28:20

Though I have fallen, I will rise. Though I sit in
darkness, the LORD will be my light.

MICAH 7:8

His mercy extends to those who fear him, from
generation to generation.

LUKE 1:50

God, who has called you into fellowship with his
Son Jesus Christ our Lord, is faithful.

1 CORINTHIANS 1:9

COURAGE

An anxious heart weighs a man down, but a kind word cheers him up.

PROVERBS 12:25

My mouth would encourage you; comfort from my lips would bring you relief.

JOB 16:5

The LORD is my light and my salvation—whom shall I fear? The LORD is the stronghold of my life—of whom shall I be afraid?

PSALM 27:1

Wait for the LORD; be strong and take heart and wait for the LORD.

PSALM 27:14

Do not fear, for I am with you; do not be dismayed, for I am your God. I will strengthen you and help you; I will uphold you with my righteous right hand.

ISAIAH 41:10

I can do everything through him who gives me strength.

PHILIPPIANS 4:13

THE COURAGE TO TRUST

After a long and terrifying captivity, Iranian hostage Gary Lee was home. It was a Sunday morning in February 1981, and I joined with others in his father's church to welcome him. Celebration filled the air as joyful voices sang "Amazing Grace." From my seat I noticed the bearded young man smile and shake his head as though in wonder at the miracle of his safe return.

Months earlier, however, he had experienced another miracle. Shortly after his capture he was allowed to have a Bible and one day he read Isaiah 43:5: "Do not be afraid, for I am with you; I will bring your children from the east and gather you from the west."

"When I read those words," he told his father later, "I felt God was making me a promise. Somehow I knew I would reach home safely. The whole experience became a lot easier after that."

How much lighter trials become when we realize God's grace is twofold. It is not only the happy ending. It is also the peace we can feel during a painful journey, when we trust in God—all the way.

Dᴏʀɪs Hᴀᴀsᴇ

Cast your cares on the LORD and he will sustain you; he will never let the righteous fall.

PSALM 55:22

You are my hiding place; you will protect me from trouble and surround me with songs of deliverance.

PSALM 32:7

In my alarm I said, "I am cut off from your sight!" Yet you heard my cry for mercy when I called to you for help . . . Be strong and take heart, all you who hope in the LORD.

PSALM 31:22, 24

My soul is downcast within me. Yet this I call to mind and therefore I have hope: Because of the LORD's great love we are not consumed, for his compassions never fail. They are new every morning; great is your faithfulness.

LAMENTATIONS 3:20–23

Why are you downcast, O my soul? Why so disturbed within me? Put your hope in God, for I will yet praise him, my Savior and my God.

PSALM 42:5–6

Let the morning bring me word of your unfailing love, for I have put my trust in you. Show me the way I should go, for to you I lift up my soul.

PSALM 143:8

The LORD is a refuge for the oppressed, a stronghold in times of trouble.

PSALM 9:9

God is our refuge and strength, an ever-present help in trouble. Therefore we will not fear, though the earth give way and the mountains fall into the heart of the sea, though its waters roar and foam and the mountains quake with their surging.

PSALM 46:1–3

My soul finds rest in God alone; my salvation comes from him. He alone is my rock and my salvation; he is my fortress, I will never be shaken.

PSALM 62:1–2

Jesus said, "I have told you these things, so that in me you may have peace. In this world you will have trouble. But take heart! I have overcome the world."

JOHN 16:33

My flesh and my heart may fail, but God is the strength of my heart and my portion forever.

PSALM 73:26

When I said, "My foot is slipping," your love, O LORD, supported me. When anxiety was great within me, your consolation brought joy to my soul.

PSALM 94:18–19

The LORD upholds all those who fall and lifts up all who are bowed down.

PSALM 145:14

Jesus said, "Come to me, all you who are weary and burdened, and I will give you rest. Take my yoke upon you and learn from me, for I am gentle and humble in heart, and you will find rest for your souls."

MATTHEW 11:28–29

God gives strength to the weary and increases the power of the weak. Even youths grow tired and weary, and young men stumble and fall; but those who hope in the LORD will renew their strength. They will soar on wings like eagles; they will run and not grow weary, they will walk and not be faint.

ISAIAH 40:29–31

I am the LORD, your God, who takes hold of your right hand and says to you, Do not fear; I will help you.

ISAIAH 41:13

When you pass through the waters, I will be with you; and when you pass through the rivers, they will not sweep over you. When you walk through the fire, you will not be burned; the flames will not set you ablaze.

ISAIAH 43:2

Jesus said, "Peace I leave with you; my peace I give you. I do not give to you as the world gives. Do not let your hearts be troubled and do not be afraid."

JOHN 14:27

Cast all your anxiety on him because he cares for you.

1 PETER 5:7

Blessed are you who hunger now, for you will be satisfied. Blessed are you who weep now, for you will laugh.

LUKE 6:21

Jesus said, "My grace is sufficient for you, for my power is made perfect in weakness."

2 CORINTHIANS 12:9

Let us not give up meeting together, as some are in the habit of doing, but let us encourage one another.

HEBREWS 10:25

May our Lord Jesus Christ himself and God our Father, who loved us and by his grace gave us eternal encouragement and good hope, encourage your hearts and strengthen you in every good deed and word.

2 THESSALONIANS 2:16–17

Encourage the timid, help the weak, be patient with everyone.

1 THESSALONIANS 5:14

"I know the plans I have for you," declares the LORD, "plans to prosper you and not to harm you, plans to give you hope and a future."

JEREMIAH 29:11

Encouragement

Getting Rid of Discouragement

After a day of dealing with a cranky baby or a hostile teenager or a demanding boss or an unsatisfied husband . . . I can say—no shout—with Elijah, "I've had enough, Lord!" (1 Kings 19:4).

If I'll just follow the Lord's prescription for discouragement, I should be able to regain control of myself and my emotions:

1) Get enough rest (1 Kings 19:5). Ever notice how a short temper is directly related to a short night's sleep? Sometimes short nights cannot be helped (infants must be fed), but as much as possible get a good night's rest.

2) Eat healthy foods on a regular basis (1 Kings 19:6). Five fingerlicks of raw cookie dough do not a healthy lunch make. Foods high in protein and low in sugar will give you the strength you need for the strains of your day.

3) Spend some quiet time with yourself and the Lord (1 Kings 19:12). There's just no getting around it. No matter how busy you are, time alone with yourself and with your Lord will provide the stability to catch and handle whatever life throws your way.

JEAN E. SYSWERDA

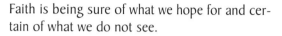
Faith is being sure of what we hope for and certain of what we do not see.

HEBREWS 11:1

Faith comes from hearing the message, and the message is heard through the word of Christ.

ROMANS 10:17

Abram believed the LORD, and he credited it to him as righteousness.

GENESIS 15:6

Let us fix our eyes on Jesus, the author and perfecter of our faith, who for the joy set before him endured the cross, scorning its shame, and sat down at the right hand of the throne of God.

HEBREWS 12:2

Jesus said, "I tell you the truth, if you have faith as small as a mustard seed, you can say to this mountain, 'Move from here to there' and it will move. Nothing will be impossible for you."

MATTHEW 17:20

Jesus touched their eyes and said, "According to your faith will it be done to you."

MATTHEW 9:29

"Have faith in God," Jesus answered. "I tell you the truth, if anyone says to this mountain, 'Go, throw yourself into the sea,' and does not doubt in his heart but believes that what he says will happen, it will be done for him. Therefore I tell you, whatever you ask for in prayer, believe that you have received it, and it will be yours."

MARK 11:22–24

In the gospel a righteousness from God is revealed, a righteousness that is by faith from first to last, just as it is written: "The righteous will live by faith."

ROMANS 1:17

We live by faith, not by sight.

2 CORINTHIANS 5:7

Without faith it is impossible to please God, because anyone who comes to him must believe that he exists and that he rewards those who earnestly seek him.

HEBREWS 11:6

We have been justified through faith.

ROMANS 5:1

Though you have not seen Christ, you love him; and even though you do not see him now, you believe in him and are filled with an inexpressible and glorious joy, for you are receiving the goal of your faith, the salvation of your souls.

1 Peter 1:8–9

A woman who had been subject to bleeding for twelve years came up behind him and touched the edge of his cloak. She said to herself, "If I only touch his cloak, I will be healed." Jesus turned and saw her. "Take heart, daughter," he said, "your faith has healed you." And the woman was healed from that moment.

Matthew 9:20–22

It is by grace you have been saved, through faith—and this not from yourselves, it is the gift of God.

Ephesians 2:8

Everyone born of God overcomes the world. This is the victory that has overcome the world, even our faith.

1 John 5:4

THE WAY OF FAITH

God is ever seeking to teach us the way of faith, and in our training in the faith life there must be room for the trial of faith, the discipline of faith, the patience of faith, the courage of faith; and often many stages are passed before we really realize what is the end of faith, namely, the victory of faith.

Real moral fiber is developed through discipline of faith. You have made your request of God, but the answer does not come. What are you to do?

Keep on believing God's Word; never be moved away from it by what you see or feel, and thus as you stand steady, enlarged power and experience is being developed. Often God delays purposely, and the delay is just as much an answer to your prayer as is the fulfillment when it comes.

Abraham, Moses and Elijah were not great in the beginning, but were made great through the discipline of their faith, and only thus were they fitted for the positions to which God had called them.

When God has spoken of his purpose to do, and yet the days go on and he does not do it, that is truly hard; but it is a discipline of faith that will bring us into a knowledge of God which would otherwise be impossible.

MRS. CHARLES E. COWMAN

FINANCES

No one can serve two masters. Either he will hate the one and love the other, or he will be devoted to the one and despise the other. You cannot serve both God and Money.

MATTHEW 6:24

Turn my heart toward your statutes and not toward selfish gain.

PSALM 119:36

Whoever trusts in his riches will fall, but the righteous will thrive like a green leaf.

PROVERBS 11:28

The LORD is my shepherd, I shall not be in want.

PSALM 23:1

Godliness with contentment is great gain. For we brought nothing into the world, and we can take nothing out of it. But if we have food and clothing, we will be content with that. People who want to get rich fall into temptation and a trap and into many foolish and harmful desires that plunge men into ruin and destruction. For the love of money is a root of all kinds of evil. Some people, eager for money, have wandered from the faith and pierced themselves with many griefs.

1 TIMOTHY 6:6–10

I know what it is to be in need, and I know what
it is to have plenty. I have learned the secret of
being content in any and every situation,
whether well fed or hungry, whether living in
plenty or in want.

PHILIPPIANS 4:12

Jesus sat down opposite the place where the
offerings were put and watched the crowd putting
their money into the temple treasury. Many rich
people threw in large amounts. But a poor widow
came and put in two very small copper coins,
worth only a fraction of a penny. Calling his disciples to him, Jesus said, "I tell you the truth, this
poor widow has put more into the treasury than
all the others. They all gave out of their wealth;
but she, out of her poverty, put in everything—all
she had to live on."

MARK 12:41–44

"Bring the whole tithe into the storehouse, that
there may be food in my house. Test me in this,"
says the LORD Almighty, "and see if I will not
throw open the floodgates of heaven and pour out
so much blessing that you will not have room
enough for it."

MALACHI 3:10

Be on your guard against all kinds of greed; a man's life does not consist in the abundance of his possessions.

LUKE 12:15

Let no debt remain outstanding, except the continuing debt to love one another, for he who loves his fellowman has fulfilled the law.

ROMANS 13:8

Jesus said, "Do not worry, saying, 'What shall we eat?' or 'What shall we drink?' or 'What shall we wear?' For the pagans run after all these things, and your heavenly Father knows that you need them. But seek first his kingdom and his righteousness, and all these things will be given to you as well."

MATTHEW 6:31–33

A good man leaves an inheritance for his children's children, but a sinner's wealth is stored up for the righteous.

PROVERBS 13:22

Remember the LORD your God, for it is he who gives you the ability to produce wealth, and so confirms his covenant, which he swore to your forefathers, as it is today.

DEUTERONOMY 8:18

SOLOMON'S FINANCES

I picked up a newspaper the other day and saw that, according to the latest statistics, our family has just pulled out of the poverty level. I had never realized our financial state of affairs was so poor.

In spite of what statistics say, we aren't forced to do without clothes, we enjoy three square meals a day, and the roof over our head is paid for, even if we shingled it ourselves. Now, the experts tell me we have only been subsisting. I wonder what real living is like?

For some people in this world, poverty is a stark reality. For others, it's just a state of mind. How disturbed should we be if our income falls below the national average, or even below the neighbor's? There is always the possibility that I am poor because I feel poor, not because I lack necessities.

Rather than striving to obtain a better standard of living by simply making more money, perhaps I need to adjust my attitude toward spending. If we are sincerely willing to try to stay within the amounts God has allotted us, I believe he will honor our efficiency.

Now and then it is wise to go over the budget systematically, bearing in mind Solomon's wise advice: "Give me neither poverty nor riches, but give me only my daily bread" (Proverbs 30:8).

ALMA BARKMAN

As far as the east is from the west, so far has he removed our transgressions from us.

PSALM 103:12

"Come now, let us reason together," says the LORD. "Though your sins are like scarlet, they shall be as white as snow; though they are red as crimson, they shall be like wool."

ISAIAH 1:18

I, even I, am he who blots out your transgressions, for my own sake, and remembers your sins no more.

ISAIAH 43:25

Once you were alienated from God and were enemies in your minds because of your evil behavior. But now he has reconciled you by Christ's physical body through death to present you holy in his sight, without blemish and free from accusation.

COLOSSIANS 1:21-22

If my people, who are called by my name, will humble themselves and pray and seek my face and turn from their wicked ways, then will I hear from heaven and will forgive their sin and will heal their land.

2 CHRONICLES 7:14

God's Words of Life on
FORGIVENESS

In him we have redemption through his blood, the forgiveness of sins, in accordance with the riches of God's grace that he lavished on us with all wisdom and understanding.

EPHESIANS 1:7-8

Who is a God like you, who pardons sin and forgives the transgression of the remnant of his inheritance? You do not stay angry forever but delight to show mercy.

MICAH 7:18

Blessed are they whose transgressions are forgiven, whose sins are covered. Blessed is the man whose sin the Lord will never count against him.

ROMANS 4:7-8

If we confess our sins, he is faithful and just and will forgive us our sins and purify us from all unrighteousness.

1 JOHN 1:9

Repent, then, and turn to God, so that your sins may be wiped out, that times of refreshing may come from the Lord, and that he may send the Christ, who has been appointed for you—even Jesus.

ACTS 3:19-20

GOD'S WORDS OF LIFE ON
FORGIVENESS

The Lord our God is merciful and forgiving, even though we have rebelled against him.

DANIEL 9:9

Praise the LORD, O my soul, and forget not all his benefits—who forgives all your sins and heals all your diseases.

PSALM 103:2-3

Forgive us our debts, as we also have forgiven our debtors. And lead us not into temptation, but deliver us from the evil one.

MATTHEW 6:12-13

He who conceals his sins does not prosper, but whoever confesses and renounces them finds mercy.

PROVERBS 28:13

For the sake of your name, O LORD, forgive my iniquity, though it is great.

PSALM 25:11

If you forgive men when they sin against you, your heavenly Father will also forgive you. But if you do not forgive men their sins, your Father will not forgive your sins.

MATTHEW 6:14-15

Be kind and compassionate to one another, forgiving each other, just as in Christ God forgave you.

EPHESIANS 4:32

Jesus said, "Do not judge, and you will not be judged. Do not condemn, and you will not be condemned. Forgive, and you will be forgiven."

LUKE 6:37

My dear children, I write this to you so that you will not sin. But if anybody does sin, we have one who speaks to the Father in our defense—Jesus Christ, the Righteous One.

1 JOHN 2:1

I will forgive their wickedness and will remember their sins no more.

HEBREWS 8:12

I will cleanse them from all the sin they have committed against me and will forgive all their sins of rebellion against me.

JEREMIAH 33:8

There is now no condemnation for those who are in Christ Jesus.

ROMANS 8:1

O Lord, hear my voice.
  Let your ears be attentive
    to my cry for mercy.
If you, O LORD, kept a record of sins,
    O Lord, who could stand?
But with you there is forgiveness;
    therefore you are feared.
I wait for the LORD, my soul waits,
    and in his word I put my hope.

PSALM 130:2–5

Help us, O God our Savior, for the glory of your name; deliver us and forgive our sins for your name's sake.

PSALM 79:9

Forgive us our sins, for we also forgive everyone who sins against us.

LUKE 11:4

❧〰

SPIRITUAL HOUSECLEANING

Much that we keep stored in boxes is not valuable to anyone but us. Ticket stubs, blackened corsages, graduation programs are worthless. Yet we keep collecting, preserving memories of important occasions.

There are happy memories and sad ones. Perhaps some bitter ones. We remember angry words and hurt feelings. The relative who didn't come to our wedding. The daughter-in-law who told us to stop interfering. We keep these in our mental storage boxes, getting them out from time to time and reliving the experience.

In Isaiah 43:25 God says to his people, "I, even I, am he who blots out your transgressions, for my own sake, and remembers your sins no more." All those terrible things we have done—God cancels them, wipes them out. He doesn't stuff them away in a drawer just in case he wants to drag them out to jog his memory. He obliterates them. He can't remember them any more. God forgives and forgets. And so should we.

As we get older we can get careless about our spiritual housekeeping. Emotional trash can collect. This is a good day to confess it, make amends and enjoy life free from ugly clutter.

JEAN SHAW

God's Words of Life on
God's Control

The LORD your God is God of gods and LORD of lords, the great God, mighty and awesome, who shows no partiality and accepts no bribes.

DEUTERONOMY 10:17

The earth is the LORD's, and everything in it, the world, and all who live in it.

PSALM 24:1

Great is the LORD and most worthy of praise; he is to be feared above all gods.

1 CHRONICLES 16:25

The LORD will reign for ever and ever.

EXODUS 15:18

God was given authority, glory and sovereign power; all peoples, nations and men of every language worshiped him. His dominion is an everlasting dominion that will not pass away, and his kingdom is one that will never be destroyed.

DANIEL 7:14

God's kingdom will be an everlasting kingdom, and all rulers will worship and obey him.

DANIEL 7:27

The LORD your God is God in heaven above and on the earth below.

JOSHUA 2:11

Dominion and awe belong to God; he establishes order in the heights of heaven.

JOB 25:2

Let them know that you, whose name is the LORD—that you alone are the Most High over all the earth.

PSALM 83:18

The LORD is our judge, the LORD is our lawgiver, the LORD is our king; it is he who will save us.

ISAIAH 33:22

I am the first and I am the last; apart from me there is no God.

ISAIAH 44:6

"I am the Alpha and the Omega," says the Lord God, "who is, and who was, and who is to come, the Almighty."

REVELATION 1:8

The Most High is sovereign over the kingdoms of men.

DANIEL 4:17

Jesus said, "Heaven and earth will pass away, but my words will never pass away."

MATTHEW 24:35

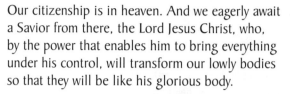

Our citizenship is in heaven. And we eagerly await a Savior from there, the Lord Jesus Christ, who, by the power that enables him to bring everything under his control, will transform our lowly bodies so that they will be like his glorious body.

PHILIPPIANS 3:20–21

The plans of the LORD stand firm forever,
the purposes of his heart through all generations.

PSALM 33:11

The mind controlled by the Spirit is life and peace.

ROMANS 8:6

The Architect of Our Lives

An African story is told about a sculptor who was sculpting the face of the king. Every day the sculptor worked on the stone, and every evening a man would come to clean away the chips. Soon this man began to see a face emerging from the rock. Finally, when the image was full and everyone could see it, he was so amazed and astonished that he went to the sculptor and asked, "How did you know the king was in that stone?"

Without a doubt, the sculptor and architect must possess the ability to design and create mentally what does not exist, and then make it reality.

Consider that God the Great Sculptor and Architect designed and created everything that exists. Not only did he make us physically, but he created faith in us. And any attempt to build our lives without God is futile and our labor is in vain. For God is the Master Builder. Without him, we can do nothing.

"Lord God, who created the world and all that is in it, I acknowledge that I am your creation. Help me to understand that anything I try to do without you is done in vain. Amen."

Reverend Rosalyn Grant Frederick

Look at the birds of the air; they do not sow or reap or store away in barns, and yet your heavenly Father feeds them. Are you not much more valuable than they?

MATTHEW 6:26

Do not be afraid, little flock, for your Father has been pleased to give you the kingdom.

LUKE 12:32

Jesus said, "I am the good shepherd. The good shepherd lays down his life for the sheep."

JOHN 10:11

Jesus said, "My sheep listen to my voice; I know them, and they follow me. I give them eternal life, and they shall never perish; no one can snatch them out of my hand. My Father, who has given them to me, is greater than all; no one can snatch them out of my Father's hand."

JOHN 10:27-29

Praise the LORD, O my soul, and forget not all his benefits—who forgives all your sins and heals all your diseases, who redeems your life from the pit and crowns you with love and compassion, who satisfies your desires with good things so that your youth is renewed like the eagle's.

PSALM 103:2-5

God's Protection

The Lord is faithful, and he will strengthen and protect you from the evil one.

2 Thessalonians 3:3

Jesus said, "I will remain in the world no longer, but they are still in the world, and I am coming to you. Holy Father, protect them by the power of your name—the name you gave me—so that they may be one as we are one."

John 17:11

Do not withhold your mercy from me, O Lord;
may your love and your truth always protect me.

Psalm 40:11

He who dwells in the shelter of the Most High will rest in the shadow of the Almighty.

Psalm 91:1

The Lord will keep you from all harm—he will watch over your life; the Lord will watch over your coming and going both now and forevermore.

Psalm 121:7-8

The Lord will be your confidence and will keep your foot from being snared.

Proverbs 3:26

GOD'S PROTECTION

Even though I walk through the valley of the shadow of death, I will fear no evil, for you are with me; your rod and your staff, they comfort me.

PSALM 23:4

Do not fear, for I am with you; do not be dismayed, for I am your God. I will strengthen you and help you; I will uphold you with my righteous right hand.

ISAIAH 41:10

Fear not, for I have redeemed you; I have summoned you by name; you are mine. When you pass through the waters, I will be with you; and when you pass through the rivers, they will not sweep over you. When you walk through the fire, you will not be burned; the flames will not set you ablaze. For I am the LORD, your God, the Holy One of Israel, your Savior.

ISAIAH 43:1-3

Jesus said, "Surely I am with you always, to the very end of the age."

MATTHEW 28:20

Surely this is our God; we trusted in him, and he saved us. This is the LORD, we trusted in him; let us rejoice and be glad in his salvation.

ISAIAH 25:9

PROTECTION IN NEW BEGINNINGS

A single, lonely bird hovered over a submerged world. Below her were the results of the catastrophic flood. The world below her was desolate and seemingly without a future. Nowhere could she find a place to hold on to, to set down her tiny foot. She found no rest.

Yet the dove that fluttered around purposelessly was less lonely than she appeared to be. Noah—his name means "he who will bring rest"—had not forgotten her. He waited for her return. When the bird came, she found an outstretched hand, ready to take her into the safety of the ark.

We can be compared with this dove. We feel lonely and forsaken. We flutter around in a world that increasingly offers less to hold onto in every way. We see little hope for humanity. Spiritually and emotionally we find no rest.

Yet there is Someone who cares about us, who watches closely for each individual: God! Through him we can find rest in spite of the catastrophes that harass the world. He offers us a place to stand, and hope, even in an apparently lost world. He offers a new beginning to those of us who return to him.

GIEN KARSSEN

Praise the LORD. Give thanks to the LORD, for he is good; his love endures forever.

PSALM 106:1

Then Hannah prayed and said:
"My heart rejoices in the LORD;
    in the LORD my horn is lifted high.
My mouth boasts over my enemies,
    for I delight in your deliverance.

1 SAMUEL 2:1

Give thanks to the LORD, for he is good; his love endures forever.

PSALM 118:1

I will extol the LORD at all times; his praise will always be on my lips.

PSALM 34:1

Do not be anxious about anything, but in everything, by prayer and petition, with thanksgiving, present your requests to God.

PHILIPPIANS 4:6

Give thanks in all circumstances, for this is God's will for you in Christ Jesus.

1 THESSALONIANS 5:18

Thanks be to God! He gives us the victory through our Lord Jesus Christ.

1 Corinthians 15:57

Thanks be to God for his indescribable gift!

2 Corinthians 9:15

Give thanks to the Lord, call on his name; make known among the nations what he has done.

1 Chronicles 16:8

Praise the Lord. I will extol the Lord with all my heart in the council of the upright and in the assembly. Great are the works of the Lord; they are pondered by all who delight in them.

Psalm 111:1–2

Sing and make music in your heart to the Lord, always giving thanks to God the Father for everything, in the name of our Lord Jesus Christ.

Ephesians 5:19–20

Rooted and built up in him, strengthened in the faith as you were taught, and overflowing with thankfulness.

Colossians 2:7

Sing to the LORD with thanksgiving; make music to our God on the harp.

PSALM 147:7

Enter his gates with thanksgiving and his courts with praise; give thanks to him and praise his name.

PSALM 100:4

Give thanks to the LORD, for he is good. His love endures forever. Give thanks to the God of gods. His love endures forever. Give thanks to the Lord of lords: His love endures forever.

PSALM 136:1–3

I will sacrifice a thank offering to you and call on the name of the LORD.

PSALM 116:17

Taking the five loaves and the two fish and looking up to heaven, Jesus gave thanks and broke them. Then he gave them to the disciples to set before the people.

LUKE 9:16

Everything God created is good, and nothing is to be rejected if it is received with thanksgiving.

1 TIMOTHY 4:4

Through Jesus, therefore, let us continually offer
to God a sacrifice of praise—the fruit of lips that
confess his name.

HEBREWS 13:15

Give thanks to the LORD, for he is good; his love
endures forever. Let the redeemed of the LORD say
this.

PSALM 107:1–2

We always thank God for all of you, mentioning you
in our prayers. We continually remember before
our God and Father your work produced by faith,
your labor prompted by love, and your endurance
inspired by hope in our Lord Jesus Christ.

1 THESSALONIANS 1:2–3

Amen! Praise and glory and wisdom and thanks
and honor and power and strength be to our God
for ever and ever. Amen!

REVELATION 7:12

I will give thanks to the LORD because of
        his righteousness
    and will sing praise to the name of the LORD
        Most High.

PSALM 7:17

61

GRATITUDE

Give thanks to the LORD for his unfailing love
and his wonderful deeds.

PSALM 107:21

Come, let us sing for joy to the LORD;
let us shout aloud to the Rock of our salvation.
Let us come before him with thanksgiving
and extol him with music and song.
For the LORD is the great God,
the great King above all gods.

PSALM 95:1–3

You turned my wailing into dancing;
you removed my sackcloth and clothed me
with joy,
that my heart may sing to you and not be silent.
O LORD my God, I will give you thanks forever.

PSALM 30:11–12

The grace that is reaching more and more people
may cause thanksgiving to overflow to the glory of
God.

2 CORINTHIANS 4:15

God will make her deserts like Eden, her waste-
lands like the garden of the LORD. Joy and gladness will be found in her, thanksgiving and the
sound of singing.

ISAIAH 51:3

Gratitude

In Everything Give Thanks

How can we have thankful, contented hearts when the circumstances in our lives are not what we had planned and when they lie outside our control or our power to change?

Let's look at our alternatives. If we are not thankful, we become bitter and angry with God: he is not providing what we "rightfully" deserve. If we are not content, we become rebellious and complaining: after all, he gives our friends everything they pray for—why does he refuse us?

Underlying these complaints and questions lie two errors in our thinking: that God is not trustworthy and that he does not desire our good. When we compare these conclusions with Scripture, we discover how wrong we are! God's Word instructs us that God is sovereignly in control. He is intimately involved with us; he works out his purposes through the events in our lives so that we may be conformed to the image of his Son.

God's love for his people is not determined by the circumstances in our lives. His love is steadfast. Our marital status, career or finances might fluctuate or totally break apart. In spite of that, however, we can and must give him thanks for his love toward us.

Carol L. Baldwin

GRIEF

All the days of my hard service I will wait for my renewal to come.

JOB 14:14

If only for this life we have hope in Christ, we are to be pitied more than all men. But Christ has indeed been raised from the dead, the firstfruits of those who have fallen asleep. For since death came through a man, the resurrection of the dead comes also through a man. For as in Adam all die, so in Christ all will be made alive.

1 CORINTHIANS 15:19–22

I tell you a mystery: We will not all sleep, but we will all be changed—in a flash, in the twinkling of an eye, at the last trumpet. For the trumpet will sound, the dead will be raised imperishable, and we will be changed. For the perishable must clothe itself with the imperishable, and the mortal with immortality. When the perishable has been clothed with the imperishable, and the mortal with immortality, then the saying that is written will come true: "Death has been swallowed up in victory." "Where, O death, is your victory? Where, O death, is your sting?"

1 CORINTHIANS 15:51–55

We believe that Jesus died and rose again and so we believe that God will bring with Jesus those who have fallen asleep in him. According to the Lord's own word, we tell you that we who are still alive, who are left till the coming of the Lord, will certainly not precede those who have fallen asleep. For the Lord himself will come down from heaven, with a loud command, with the voice of the archangel and with the trumpet call of God, and the dead in Christ will rise first. After that, we who are still alive and are left will be caught up together with them in the clouds to meet the Lord in the air. And so we will be with the Lord forever. Therefore encourage each other with these words.

1 THESSALONIANS 4:14–18

I heard a loud voice from the throne saying, "Now the dwelling of God is with men, and he will live with them. They will be his people, and God himself will be with them and be their God. He will wipe every tear from their eyes. There will be no more death or mourning or crying or pain, for the old order of things has passed away."

REVELATION 21:3–4

Even though I walk through the valley of the shadow of death, I will fear no evil, for you are with me; your rod and your staff, they comfort me.

PSALM 23:4

Into your hands I commit my spirit; redeem me, O LORD, the God of truth.

PSALM 31:5

Multitudes who sleep in the dust of the earth will awake: some to everlasting life, others to shame and everlasting contempt. Those who are wise will shine like the brightness of the heavens, and those who lead many to righteousness, like the stars for ever and ever.

DANIEL 12:2–3

You guide me with your counsel, and afterward you will take me into glory. Whom have I in heaven but you? And earth has nothing I desire besides you. My flesh and my heart may fail, but God is the strength of my heart and my portion forever.

PSALM 73:24–26

Precious in the sight of the LORD is the death of his saints.

PSALM 116:15

Those who walk uprightly enter into peace; they find rest as they lie in death.

ISAIAH 57:2

For none of us lives to himself alone and none of us dies to himself alone. If we live, we live to the Lord; and if we die, we die to the Lord. So, whether we live or die, we belong to the Lord.

ROMANS 14:7–8

Now we know that if the earthly tent we live in is destroyed, we have a building from God, an eternal house in heaven, not built by human hands.

2 CORINTHIANS 5:1

We are confident, I say, and would prefer to be away from the body and at home with the Lord.

2 CORINTHIANS 5:8

For to me, to live is Christ and to die is gain.

PHILIPPIANS 1:21

He died for us so that, whether we are awake or asleep, we may live together with him.

1 THESSALONIANS 5:10

Now there is in store for me the crown of righteousness, which the Lord, the righteous Judge, will award to me on that day—and not only to me, but also to all who have longed for his appearing.

2 TIMOTHY 4:8

He too shared in their humanity so that by his death he might destroy him who holds the power of death—that is, the devil—and free those who all their lives were held in slavery by their fear of death.

HEBREWS 2:14–15

I heard a voice from heaven say, "Write: Blessed are the dead who die in the Lord from now on." "Yes," says the Spirit, "they will rest from their labor, for their deeds will follow them."

REVELATION 14:13

If Christ is in you, your body is dead because of sin, yet your spirit is alive because of righteousness. And if the Spirit of him who raised Jesus from the dead is living in you, he who raised Christ from the dead will also give life to your mortal bodies through his Spirit, who lives in you.

ROMANS 8:10–11

We who have fled to take hold of the hope offered to us may be greatly encouraged. We have this hope as an anchor for the soul, firm and secure.

HEBREWS 6:18–19

Blessed are those who mourn, for they will be comforted.

MATTHEW 5:4

GOD'S WORDS OF LIFE ON

GRIEF

Hear, O LORD, and be merciful to me; O LORD, be my help.

PSALM 30:10

Let everyone who is godly pray to you while you may be found; surely when the mighty waters rise, they will not reach him. You are my hiding place; you will protect me from trouble and surround me with songs of deliverance.

PSALM 32:6–7

I waited patiently for the LORD; he turned to me and heard my cry. He lifted me out of the slimy pit, out of the mud and mire; he set my feet on a rock and gave me a firm place to stand. He put a new song in my mouth, a hymn of praise to our God.

PSALM 40:1–3

This is what the LORD says: "Restrain your voice from weeping and your eyes from tears . . . there is hope for your future," declares the LORD.

JEREMIAH 31:16–17

Just as the sufferings of Christ flow over into our lives, so also through Christ our comfort overflows.

2 CORINTHIANS 1:5

GOD'S WORDS OF LIFE ON
GRIEF

Jesus said, "You will grieve, but your grief will turn to joy."

JOHN 16:20

I will turn their mourning into gladness; I will give them comfort and joy instead of sorrow.

JEREMIAH 31:13

He will swallow up death forever. The Sovereign LORD will wipe away the tears from all faces.

ISAIAH 25:8

Those who sow in tears will reap with songs of joy. He who goes out weeping, carrying seed to sow, will return with songs of joy, carrying sheaves with him.

PSALM 126:5–6

Everlasting joy will crown their heads. Gladness and joy will overtake them, and sorrow and sighing will flee away.

ISAIAH 35:10

THE WORK OF GRIEF

I discovered after the death of my husband Jim that grieving is work: exhausting and regressive. I found it didn't progress in neat and predictable stages but was frustratingly erratic and repetitive. As I stepped aside periodically to evaluate, I saw improvement overall: a gradual lessening of the pain and fear, a growing confidence in my ability to handle life's everydayness.

But setbacks were sudden and frequent those first months. I would often find terrain which I thought I had traversed and left behind me was maddeningly underfoot again. I tried to learn to evaluate life in bigger chunks. Looking back over a month's progress can be more encouraging than too-frequent scrutiny.

In looking back over that first year of deliberate grief work, I began to see patterns in my choices and a new principle about life began to take shape in my mind. The principle is this: beauty can help to bring healing. I am convinced that God has built into all of us, in varying degrees, the capacity for an appreciation of beauty. It may be one way God brings healing to our brokenness, and a way that we can contribute toward bringing wholeness to our fallen world.

MARY JANE WORDEN

If any of you lacks wisdom, he should ask God, who gives generously to all without finding fault, and it will be given to him.

JAMES 1:5

I will instruct you and teach you in the way you should go; I will counsel you and watch over you.

PSALM 32:8

Whether you turn to the right or to the left, your ears will hear a voice behind you, saying, "This is the way; walk in it."

ISAIAH 30:21

This God is our God for ever and ever; he will be our guide even to the end.

PSALM 48:14

Your word is a lamp to my feet and a light for my path.

PSALM 119:105

Commit to the LORD whatever you do, and your plans will succeed.

PROVERBS 16:3

GOD'S WORDS OF LIFE ON
GUIDANCE

Since you are my rock and my fortress, for the sake of your name lead and guide me.

PSALM 31:3

Trust in the LORD with all your heart and lean not on your own understanding; in all your ways acknowledge him, and he will make your paths straight.

PROVERBS 3:5–6

The LORD will guide you always; he will satisfy your needs in a sun-scorched land and will strengthen your frame. You will be like a well-watered garden, like a spring whose waters never fail.

ISAIAH 58:11

Jesus said, "When he, the Spirit of truth, comes, he will guide you into all truth."

JOHN 16:13

Show me your ways, O LORD, teach me your paths.

PSALM 25:4

You are my lamp, O LORD; the LORD turns my darkness into light.

2 SAMUEL 22:29

The LORD gives wisdom, and from his mouth
come knowledge and understanding.

PROVERBS 2:6

"I know the plans I have for you," declares the
LORD, "plans to prosper you and not to harm you,
plans to give you hope and a future."

JEREMIAH 29:11

It is God who works in you to will and to act
according to his good purpose.

PHILIPPIANS 2:13

He restores my soul. He guides me in paths of
righteousness for his name's sake.

PSALM 23:3

I am always with you;
    you hold me by my right hand.
You guide me with your counsel,
    and afterward you will take me into glory.

PSALM 73:23–24

He brought his people out like a flock;
    he led them like sheep through the desert.
He guided them safely, so they were unafraid.

PSALM 78:52–53

God will teach us his ways, so that we may walk in his paths.

ISAIAH 2:3

This is what the LORD says, he who made the earth, the LORD who formed it and established it—the LORD is his name: "Call to me and I will answer you and tell you great and unsearchable things you do not know."

JEREMIAH 33:2–3

Understanding is a fountain of life to those who have it.

PROVERBS 16:22

The path of life leads upward for the wise.

PROVERBS 15:24

In your unfailing love you will lead the people you have redeemed. In your strength you will guide them to your holy dwelling.

EXODUS 15:13

I guide you in the way of wisdom and lead you along straight paths. When you walk, your steps will not be hampered; when you run, you will not stumble.

PROVERBS 4:11–12

Guide me in your truth and teach me,
for you are God my Savior,
and my hope is in you all day long.
Remember, O LORD, your great mercy and love
for they are from of old.

PSALM 25:5–6

He guides the humble in what is right and teaches them his way.

PSALM 25:9

"I will lead the blind by ways they have not known, along unfamiliar paths I will guide them; I will turn the darkness into light before them and make the rough places smooth. These are the things I will do; I will not forsake them," says the LORD.

ISAIAH 42:16

If I rise on the wings of the dawn,
if I settle on the far side of the sea,
even there your hand will guide me,
your right hand will hold me fast, O LORD.

PSALM 139:9–10

❧

GUIDANCE OR A GUIDE?

Sometimes when we ask God our "Why" questions, instead of giving us answers he gives us himself—the Comforter. From Luke 11:13 we learn: Even as fathers give good gifts to their children, so our Father gives the best gift, the Holy Spirit, the Comforter, to us as we ask.

It reminded me of conversations with my daughter Jessie about why I wouldn't allow her to sleep over at a friend's house: "I can give you my reasons, but you won't like them or understand them, and you'd only argue with me. So let's just accept that this is the way it's going to be, and I'm sorry you feel sad."

Often when we ask God for guidance, what we really want is a guide. My friend told me of a conversation he had with his young son shortly after they moved into their new house. "You can find your way to your new bedroom in the dark by simply turning on the lights in each room as you go." There was an uncertain pause, then, "But, Daddy, won't you please go with me?"

MARY JANE WORDEN

God's Words of Life on
Holiness

Offer your bodies as living sacrifices, holy and pleasing to God—this is your spiritual act of worship. Do not conform any longer to the pattern of this world, but be transformed by the renewing of your mind. Then you will be able to test and approve what God's will is—his good, pleasing and perfect will.

ROMANS 12:1–2

Make every effort to live in peace with all men and to be holy; without holiness no one will see the LORD.

HEBREWS 12:14

God did not call us to be impure, but to live a holy life.

1 THESSALONIANS 4:7

What does the LORD your God ask of you but to fear the LORD your God, to walk in all his ways, to love him, to serve the LORD your God with all your heart and with all your soul.

DEUTERONOMY 10:12

Serve him with wholehearted devotion and with a willing mind, for the LORD searches every heart and understands every motive behind the thoughts. If you seek him, he will be found by you.

1 CHRONICLES 28:9

❧

CREATE IN ME

Create in me, Lord . . . a pure heart, yes. But Father, even more. Create in me . . . (out of nothing—for that's what creation means) an expectant heart. I stand on tiptoe waiting each moment in joyous anticipation for what you are going to do! Create in me an enthusiastic heart—en theo— meaning "in God," God in me, filled to overflowing with you, Lord! Create in me a laughing heart—one that sees the serendipities of an autumn leaf and mist upon the mountains and hears the chuckle of a child. Create in me a heart of integrity—to be real, not to talk above my walk, not to try to impress. Create in me a caring heart—tender toward the hurts and happenings of others, more concerned with their needs than with my own. Create in me an attentive heart—able to hear your whisper, and moment by moment listen to your voice. Create in me a contented heart—at peace with the circumstances of life. Create in me a hungry heart—longing to love you more, desiring your Word, reaching . . . stretching . . . for more of you. Creator Lord, create in me. Amen.

CAROLE MAYHALL

Jesus said, "I tell you the truth, anyone who gives you a cup of water in my name because you belong to Christ will certainly not lose his reward."

MARK 9:41

If you make the Most High your dwelling—even the LORD, who is my refuge—then no harm will befall you, no disaster will come near your tent.

PSALM 91:9–10

If you are pure and upright, even now he will rouse himself on your behalf and restore you to your rightful place. Your beginnings will seem humble, so prosperous will your future be.

JOB 8:6–7

All these blessings will come upon you and accompany you if you obey the LORD your God: You will be blessed in the city and blessed in the country. The fruit of your womb will be blessed, and the crops of your land and the young of your livestock—the calves of your herds and the lambs of your flocks. Your basket and your kneading trough will be blessed. You will be blessed when you come in and blessed when you go out.

DEUTERONOMY 28:2–6

The house of the righteous contains great treasure.

PROVERBS 15:6

God's Words of Life on
HOMEMAKING

By wisdom a house is built, and through understanding it is established; through knowledge its rooms are filled with rare and beautiful treasures.

PROVERBS 24:3–4

Unless the LORD builds the house, its builders labor in vain.

PSALM 127:1

Fix these words of mine in your hearts and minds; tie them as symbols on your hands and bind them on your foreheads. Teach them to your children, talking about them when you sit at home and when you walk along the road, when you lie down and when you get up. Write them on the doorframes of your houses and on your gates,

DEUTERONOMY 11:18–20

The LORD's curse is on the house of the wicked, but he blesses the home of the righteous.

PROVERBS 3:33

As for me and my household, we will serve the LORD.

JOSHUA 24:15

The LORD will open the heavens, the storehouse of his bounty, . . . to bless all the work of your hands.

DEUTERONOMY 28:12

GOD'S WORDS OF LIFE ON
HOMEMAKING

A wife of noble character who can find? She is worth far more than rubies . . . She watches over the affairs of her household and does not eat the bread of idleness. Her children arise and call her blessed; her husband also, and he praises her.

PROVERBS 31:10, 27–28

I will be careful to lead a blameless life—when will you come to me? I will walk in my house with blameless heart. I will set before my eyes no vile thing.

PSALM 101:2–3

As you come to him, the living Stone—rejected by men but chosen by God and precious to him— you also, like living stones, are being built into a spiritual house.

1 PETER 2:4–5

Every house is built by someone, but God is the builder of everything. Moses was faithful as a servant in all God's house, testifying to what would be said in the future. But Christ is faithful as a son over God's house. And we are his house, if we hold on to our courage and the hope of which we boast.

HEBREWS 3:4–6

HOMEMAKING

THE GOOD
DAYS OF HOME

It's been a good day, Lord. Yes, a very good day.
I didn't realize it while it was happening. There
were many frustrations. I was very discouraged when
the letter I was praying for didn't come. Then the
telephone rang, bringing good news.

My husband stands in the yard, leaning on his rake
as he visits with a neighbor.

Other children come spilling across the yard. The
sun is a golden glory behind the trees. I can smell
the pot roast mingling with the tangy fragrance of
burning leaves.

I look back on this day with its usual ups and downs.
Its moments of anguish, its moments of gratefulness
and joy. And now that it's ending, an aching aware-
ness fills me. I realize that it's been a good day,
Lord. A very good day.

For it's been filled with life. The life you have given
me to cope with, and to contribute to. And I wouldn't
want to have missed it, not a single moment of it.

Thank you, God, for this good day.

MARJORIE HOLMES

God's Words of Life on
Hope

Be strong and take heart, all you who hope in the LORD.

PSALM 31:24

The eyes of the LORD are on those who fear him, on those whose hope is in his unfailing love.

PSALM 33:18

Hope deferred makes the heart sick, but a longing fulfilled is a tree of life.

PROVERBS 13:12

I wait for you, O LORD; you will answer, O Lord my God.

PSALM 38:15

Faith is being sure of what we hope for and certain of what we do not see.

HEBREWS 11:1

Now, Lord, what do I look for? My hope is in you.

PSALM 39:7

Why are you downcast, O my soul? Why so disturbed within me? Put your hope in God, for I will yet praise him, my Savior and my God.

PSALM 43:5

You have been my hope, O Sovereign LORD, my confidence since my youth.

PSALM 71:5

We also rejoice in our sufferings, because we know that suffering produces perseverance; perseverance, character; and character, hope. And hope does not disappoint us, because God has poured out his love into our hearts by the Holy Spirit, whom he has given us.

ROMANS 5:3–5

As for me, I will always have hope; I will praise you more and more.

PSALM 71:14

May those who fear you rejoice when they see me, for I have put my hope in your word.

PSALM 119:74

Everything that was written in the past was written to teach us, so that through endurance and the encouragement of the Scriptures we might have hope.

ROMANS 15:4

May your unfailing love rest upon us, O LORD, even as we put our hope in you.

PSALM 33:22

Put your hope in the LORD, for with the LORD is unfailing love and with him is full redemption.

PSALM 130:7

Blessed is he whose help is the God of Jacob, whose hope is in the LORD his God, the Maker of heaven and earth, the sea, and everything in them—the LORD, who remains faithful forever.

PSALM 146:5–6

This I call to mind and therefore I have hope: Because of the LORD's great love we are not consumed, for his compassions never fail . . . The LORD is good to those whose hope is in him, to the one who seeks him.

LAMENTATIONS 3:21–22, 25

May the God of hope fill you with all joy and peace as you trust in him, so that you may overflow with hope by the power of the Holy Spirit.

ROMANS 15:13

We continually remember before our God and Father your work produced by faith, your labor prompted by love, and your endurance inspired by hope in our Lord Jesus Christ.

1 THESSALONIANS 1:3

May our Lord Jesus Christ himself and God our
Father, who loved us and by his grace gave us
eternal encouragement and good hope, encourage
your hearts and strengthen you in every good
deed and word.

2 THESSALONIANS 2:16–17

We have this hope as an anchor for the soul, firm
and secure.

HEBREWS 6:19

Always be prepared to give an answer to everyone
who asks you to give the reason for the hope that
you have.

1 PETER 3:15

Be joyful in hope, patient in affliction, faithful in
prayer.

ROMANS 12:12

Since we have been justified through faith, we
have peace with God through our Lord Jesus
Christ, through whom we have gained access by
faith into this grace in which we now stand. And
we rejoice in the hope of the glory of God.

ROMANS 5:1–2

Hope that is seen is no hope at all. Who hopes for what he already has? But if we hope for what we do not yet have, we wait for it patiently.

ROMANS 8:24–25

Why are you downcast, O my soul?
   Why so disturbed within me?
Put your hope in God,
   for I will yet praise him,
   my Savior and my God.

PSALM 42:11

Praise be to the God and Father of our Lord Jesus Christ! In his great mercy he has given us new birth into a living hope through the resurrection of Jesus Christ from the dead.

1 PETER 1:3

BE JOYFUL IN HOPE

I wondered why God asks us to be joyful in hope. I can understand why He reminds us to be faithful in prayer—so many times in hardships we slack off in prayer. I can also understand why God asks us to be patient in affliction—patience is hard to muster when you're hurting.

But why does God say to be joyful in hope? Obviously, there must be many times when we lack joy in hope. Think about it. The focus of our hope is yet to be fulfilled; we don't yet possess that for which we hope. And you'll agree that it's hard to be joyful about something we don't yet have!

Lying in bed, it hit home that God wants me to be joyful about future things. Just as we have the command to be faithful in prayer and patient in affliction, we have a command to be joyful in hope. How can God command joy? It's easy once we realize what's over the heavenly horizon.

Does the idea of heavenly glories above put a smile on your face? Do you get a charge when you talk about the return of the Lord? Heaven will seem more near and real to you as you stir up your joy over that for which you hope. And remember, it's a command for your own good.

JONI EARECKSON TADA

Jesus said, "For I was hungry and you gave me something to eat, I was thirsty and you gave me something to drink, I was a stranger and you invited me in, I needed clothes and you clothed me, I was sick and you looked after me, I was in prison and you came to visit me." Then the righteous will answer him, 'Lord, when did we see you hungry and feed you, or thirsty and give you something to drink? When did we see you a stranger and invite you in, or needing clothes and clothe you? When did we see you sick or in prison and go to visit you?' The King will reply, 'I tell you the truth, whatever you did for one of the least of these brothers of mine, you did for me.'"

MATTHEW 25:35–40

Share with God's people who are in need. Practice hospitality.

ROMANS 12:13

Then Jesus said to his host, "When you give a luncheon or dinner, do not invite your friends, your brothers or relatives, or your rich neighbors; if you do, they may invite you back and so you will be repaid. But when you give a banquet, invite the poor, the crippled, the lame, the blind, and you will be blessed. Although they cannot repay you, you will be repaid at the resurrection of the righteous."

LUKE 14:12–14

Is not this the kind of fasting I have chosen: to loose the chains of injustice and untie the cords of the yoke, to set the oppressed free and break every yoke? Is it not to share your food with the hungry and to provide the poor wanderer with shelter—when you see the naked, to clothe him, and not to turn away from your own flesh and blood? Then your light will break forth like the dawn, and your healing will quickly appear; then your righteousness will go before you, and the glory of the LORD will be your rear guard.

ISAIAH 58:6–8

Be hospitable, one who loves what is good, who is self-controlled, upright, holy and disciplined.

TITUS 1:8

Do not forget to entertain strangers, for by so doing some people have entertained angels without knowing it.

HEBREWS 13:2

Offer hospitality to one another without grumbling.

1 PETER 4:9

If anyone serves, he should do it with the strength God provides, so that in all things God may be praised through Jesus Christ.

1 PETER 4:11

Abraham looked up and saw three men standing nearby. When he saw them, he hurried from the entrance of his tent to meet them and bowed low to the ground. He said, "If I have found favor in your eyes, my lord, do not pass your servant by. Let a little water be brought, and then you may all wash your feet and rest under this tree. Let me get you something to eat, so you can be refreshed and then go on your way—now that you have come to your servant." "Very well," they answered, "do as you say."

GENESIS 18:2–5

We ought therefore to show hospitality to such men so that we may work together for the truth.

3 JOHN 8

Do not forget to do good and to share with others, for with such sacrifices God is pleased.

HEBREWS 13:16

HOSPITALITY

HOSPITALITY NEEDED, NOT WEALTH

Some of us feel that it is a lack of money that holds us down. Gideon replied to God's request, "But Lord . . . how can I save Israel? My clan is the weakest in Manasseh, and I am the least of my family" (Judges 6:15). With no finances behind him at all, Gideon was turned into a wise prophet by God's commanding power.

Many times I have had sweet Christians tell me they cannot have friends in for fellowship because they do not have good china or matching napkins, because their house is too small, or because their talent is too slight. But these are only excuses for our unwillingness to do as God has asked us. "Offer hospitality to one another without grumbling" (1 Peter 4:9). I would enjoy a peanut butter sandwich if someone else prepared it and handed it to me.

The world tells us that we need money to be happy, but as God told Gideon, "I will be with you" (Judges 6:16). Should not his presence be assurance enough?

FLORENCE LITTAUER

Light is shed upon the righteous and joy on the upright in heart.

PSALM 97:11

He will yet fill your mouth with laughter and your lips with shouts of joy.

JOB 8:21

His favor lasts a lifetime; weeping may remain for a night, but rejoicing comes in the morning.

PSALM 30:5

Rejoice in the LORD and be glad, you righteous; sing, all you who are upright in heart!

PSALM 32:11

May all who seek you rejoice and be glad in you; may those who love your salvation always say, "Let God be exalted!"

PSALM 70:4

The ransomed of the LORD will return. They will enter Zion with singing; everlasting joy will crown their heads. Gladness and joy will overtake them, and sorrow and sighing will flee away.

ISAIAH 51:11

Let all who take refuge in you be glad; let them ever sing for joy. Spread your protection over them, that those who love your name may rejoice in you.

PSALM 5:11

Shout for joy to the LORD, all the earth. Worship the LORD with gladness; come before him with joyful songs.

PSALM 100:1–2

I rejoice in following your statutes as one rejoices in great riches.

PSALM 119:14

Your statutes are my heritage forever; they are the joy of my heart.

PSALM 119:111

The prospect of the righteous is joy.

PROVERBS 10:28

You will go out in joy and be led forth in peace; the mountains and hills will burst into song before you, and all the trees of the field will clap their hands.

ISAIAH 55:12

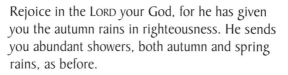

Rejoice in the LORD your God, for he has given you the autumn rains in righteousness. He sends you abundant showers, both autumn and spring rains, as before.

JOEL 2:23

Do not rejoice that the spirits submit to you, but rejoice that your names are written in heaven.

LUKE 10:20

Jesus said, "Until now you have not asked for anything in my name. Ask and you will receive, and your joy will be complete."

JOHN 16:24

Consider it pure joy, my brothers, whenever you face trials of many kinds, because you know that the testing of your faith develops perseverance.

JAMES 1:2–3

You have made known to me the paths of life; you will fill me with joy in your presence.

ACTS 2:28

The kingdom of God is not a matter of eating and drinking, but of righteousness, peace and joy in the Holy Spirit.

ROMANS 14:17

❧❧

I have spoken unto you, that my joy might remain in you, and that your joy might be full.

JOHN 15:11

Rejoice in the Lord always. I will say it again: Rejoice!

PHILIPPIANS 4:4

Be joyful always.

1 THESSALONIANS 5:16

May the God of hope fill you with all joy and peace as you trust in him, so that you may overflow with hope by the power of the Holy Spirit.

ROMANS 15:13

This day is sacred to our Lord. Do not grieve, for the joy of the LORD is your strength.

NEHEMIAH 8:10

I delight greatly in the LORD; my soul rejoices in my God. For he has clothed me with garments of salvation and arrayed me in a robe of righteousness, as a bridegroom adorns his head like a priest, and as a bride adorns herself with her jewels.

ISAIAH 61:10

GOD'S WORDS OF LIFE ON
JOY

Let the light of your face shine upon us, O LORD.
You have filled my heart with greater joy
    than when their grain and new wine abound.

PSALM 4:6–7

In him our hearts rejoice, for we trust in his
        holy name.

PSALM 33:21

Jesus said: "I will see you again and you will
rejoice, and no one will take away your joy."

JOHN 16:22

Because you are my help,
    I sing in the shadow of your wings.

PSALM 63:7

You have made known to me the path of life;
    you will fill me with joy in your presence,
    with eternal pleasures at your right hand.

PSALM 16:11

The LORD is my strength and my shield;
    my heart trusts in him, and I am helped.
My heart leaps for joy
    and I will give thanks to him in song.

PSALM 28:7

❧

The Source of Joy

We find that our joy is greatly affected by circumstances. When everything goes smoothly, we radiate a joyful spirit. But what happens when everything goes wrong, when our world seems to fall apart around us? Our joy seems to "fly out the window."

The source of true joy is the Lord himself. There is a difference between the joy that comes from peaceful circumstances and the joy of the Lord which is constant and enduring day after day regardless of the circumstances about us.

In God's Word we read of the nine Christian virtues which are the fruit of the Spirit: "But the fruit of the Spirit is love, joy, peace, patience, kindness, goodness, faithfulness, gentleness and self-control" (Galatians 5:22–23). We might illustrate this in the following way. A flower has a number of petals, and each petal is an essential part of the complete flower. Joy is one of the "petals" in the fruit of the Spirit, and without it we are not complete Christians.

The joy of the Lord transforms us and gives a cheerfulness and joyousness that is not dependent upon our outward circumstances but comes from the presence of Christ in our hearts. It has been aptly said, "Joy is the flag which is flown from the castle of the heart when the King is in residence there."

Millie Stamm

This is what the LORD Almighty says: "Administer true justice; show mercy and compassion to one another. Do not oppress the widow or the fatherless, the alien or the poor."

ZECHARIAH 7:9–10

Give to the one who asks you, and do not turn away from the one who wants to borrow from you.

MATTHEW 5:42

Carry each other's burdens, and in this way you will fulfill the law of Christ.

GALATIANS 6:2

Therefore, as we have opportunity, let us do good to all people, especially to those who belong to the family of believers.

GALATIANS 6:10

Be kind and compassionate to one another.

EPHESIANS 4:32

As God's chosen people, holy and dearly loved, clothe yourselves with compassion, kindness, humility, gentleness and patience.

COLOSSIANS 3:12

KINDNESS

At this, Ruth bowed down with her face to the ground. She exclaimed, "Why have I found such favor in your eyes that you notice me—a foreigner?" Boaz replied, "I've been told all about what you have done for your mother-in-law since the death of your husband—how you left your father and mother and your homeland and came to live with a people you did not know before. May the LORD repay you for what you have done. May you be richly rewarded by the LORD, the God of Israel, under whose wings you have come to take refuge."

RUTH 2:10–12

When the kindness and love of God our Savior appeared, he saved us, not because of righteous things we had done, but because of his mercy.

TITUS 3:4–5

Jesus said, "If anyone gives even a cup of cold water to one of these little ones because he is my disciple, I tell you the truth, he will certainly not lose his reward."

MATTHEW 10:42

Love is patient, love is kind. It does not envy, it does not boast, it is not proud.

1 CORINTHIANS 13:4

God's Words of Life on
KINDNESS

In everything, do to others what you would have them do to you, for this sums up the Law and the Prophets.

MATTHEW 7:12

May the LORD show kindness to you, as you have shown . . . to me.

RUTH 1:8

Show me unfailing kindness like that of the LORD as long as I live.

1 SAMUEL 20:14

"With everlasting kindness I will have compassion on you," says the LORD your Redeemer.

ISAIAH 54:8

The LORD is compassionate and gracious,
    slow to anger, abounding in love.
He will not always accuse,
    nor will he harbor his anger forever.

PSALM 103:8–9

❧

MEDICINE CHEST KINDNESS

Yesterday the doorbell rang, and a terrified young fellow hopping up and down on my doorstep tried to tell me that his pal was bleeding to death on the road—massive hemorrhage. I ran to the site of the accident, where the victim was just untangling himself from the wreckage of his bicycle. Judging from his groans, I thought he had amputated his leg.

Somehow I managed to get him into my bathroom and wash off his wounds. He had simply scraped the scab from a previous injury. I solemnly conjured up an impressive-looking bandage, and he was back on the road in no time at all, completely cured.

Whether it is a tiny sliver in a chubby finger, or cancer clawing at a ravaged frame, pain demands priority. Why then am I so hesitant in dispensing consolation? Must I first suffer physically, mentally, emotionally, or spiritually before I learn the healing value of a soothing hand, a mutual tear, a sympathizing heart, an understanding word?

Surely I do well to keep my medicine chest well stocked with love and compassion as well as with bandages, for I never know when I will be called upon to deal with tragedy, or when tragedy may call to deal with me.

ALMA BARKMAN

GOD'S WORDS OF LIFE ON
LISTENING

This is the confidence we have in approaching God: that if we ask anything according to his will, he hears us. And if we know that he hears us—whatever we ask—we know that we have what we asked of him.

1 JOHN 5:14–15

Listen, listen to me, and eat what is good, and your soul will delight in the richest of fare. Give ear and come to me; hear me, that your soul may live.

ISAIAH 55:2–3

Whoever listens to me will live in safety and be at ease, without fear of harm.

PROVERBS 1:33

Pay attention to my wisdom, listen well to my words of insight, that you may maintain discretion and your lips may preserve knowledge.

PROVERBS 5:1–2

As the Holy Spirit says: "Today, if you hear his voice, do not harden your hearts."

HEBREWS 3:7–8

He who listens to a life-giving rebuke will be at home among the wise.

PROVERBS 15:31

Jesus said, "Everyone who listens to the Father and learns from him comes to me."

JOHN 6:45

We are from God, and whoever knows God listens to us; but whoever is not from God does not listen to us. This is how we recognize the Spirit of truth and the spirit of falsehood.

1 JOHN 4:6

Jesus said, "Here I am! I stand at the door and knock. If anyone hears my voice and opens the door, I will come in and eat with him, and he with me."

REVELATION 3:20

Jesus said, "My sheep listen to my voice; I know them, and they follow me."

JOHN 10:27

Jesus said, "The man who enters by the gate is the shepherd of his sheep. The watchman opens the gate for him, and the sheep listen to his voice. He calls his own sheep by name and leads them out. When he has brought out all his own, he goes on ahead of them, and his sheep follow him because they know his voice."

JOHN 10:2–4

The LORD said, "Go out and stand on the mountain in the presence of the LORD, for the LORD is about to pass by." Then a great and powerful wind tore the mountains apart and shattered the rocks before the LORD, but the LORD was not in the wind. After the wind there was an earthquake, but the LORD was not in the earthquake. After the earthquake came a fire, but the LORD was not in the fire. And after the fire came a gentle whisper. When Elijah heard it, he pulled his cloak over his face and went out and stood at the mouth of the cave.

1 KINGS 19:11–13

Anyone who listens to the word but does not do what it says is like a man who looks at his face in a mirror and, after looking at himself, goes away and immediately forgets what he looks like.

JAMES 1:23–24

In the past God spoke to our forefathers through the prophets at many times and in various ways, but in these last days he has spoken to us by his Son, whom he appointed heir of all things, and through whom he made the universe.

HEBREWS 1:1–2

We must pay more careful attention, therefore, to what we have heard, so that we do not drift away.

HEBREWS 2:1

❧

STOP TALKING AND LISTEN

It happens all the time. You get together with a friend, or someone you haven't seen in a while, and before you know it, you've filled the air with a lot of talk about . . . you. You realize in embarrassment that you're rambling on about yourself and have nearly forgotten to include your friend or even God in the conversation. Oh, to be able to use words with restraint.

That's why I love traveling with my husband or my best friends. We are able to relax and be silent in each other's presence. No forced conversations. No filling the air with empty words. What a blessing it is to be able to sit with someone you love, smile at each other occasionally, and enjoy the quiet together.

When you stop talking long enough to listen, you learn something—only in silence can what you hear filter from your head into your heart. Only in silence can you hear the heartbeat of God and His still, small voice. In quiet, you realize spiritual insights that reach far beyond words.

If you meet with a friend today, make a concerted effort to talk less and listen more. It may do wonders for your friendship. And this evening when you retire, say less in your prayer time and devote more moments simply listening to God.

JONI EARECKSON TADA

Jesus said, "My command is this: Love each other as I have loved you."

JOHN 15:12

Be devoted to one another in brotherly love. Honor one another above yourselves.

ROMANS 12:10

Do not seek revenge or bear a grudge against one of your people, but love your neighbor as yourself.

LEVITICUS 19:18

Do not use your freedom to indulge the sinful nature; rather, serve one another in love. The entire law is summed up in a single command: "Love your neighbor as yourself."

GALATIANS 5:13–14

How good and pleasant it is when brothers live together in unity!

PSALM 133:1

Live a life of love, just as Christ loved us and gave himself up for us as a fragrant offering and sacrifice to God.

EPHESIANS 5:2

May the Lord make your love increase and overflow for each other and for everyone else, just as
ours does for you.

1 THESSALONIANS 3:12

You yourselves have been taught by God to love
each other.

1 THESSALONIANS 4:9

Keep on loving each other.

HEBREWS 13:1

If you really keep the royal law found in Scripture,
"Love your neighbor as yourself," you are doing
right.

JAMES 2:8

Hatred stirs up dissension, but love covers over
all wrongs.

PROVERBS 10:12

Live in harmony with one another; be sympathetic,
love as brothers, be compassionate and humble.
Do not repay evil with evil or insult with insult,
but with blessing, because to this you were called
so that you may inherit a blessing.

1 PETER 3:8–9

Jesus said, "A new command I give you: Love one another. As I have loved you, so you must love one another. By this all men will know that you are my disciples, if you love one another."

JOHN 13:34–35

Now that you have purified yourselves by obeying the truth so that you have sincere love for your brothers, love one another deeply, from the heart.

1 PETER 1:22

Let us love one another, for love comes from God. Everyone who loves has been born of God and knows God. Whoever does not love does not know God, because God is love.

1 JOHN 4:7–8

No one has ever seen God; but if we love one another, God lives in us and his love is made complete in us.

1 JOHN 4:12

He has given us this command: Whoever loves God must also love his brother.

1 JOHN 4:21

The only thing that counts is faith expressing itself through love.

GALATIANS 5:6

If I speak in the tongues of men and of angels, but have not love, I am only a resounding gong or a clanging cymbal. If I have the gift of prophecy and can fathom all mysteries and all knowledge, and if I have a faith that can move mountains, but have not love, I am nothing. If I give all I possess to the poor and surrender my body to the flames, but have not love, I gain nothing. Love is patient, love is kind. It does not envy, it does not boast, it is not proud. It is not rude, it is not self-seeking, it is not easily angered, it keeps no record of wrongs. Love does not delight in evil but rejoices with the truth. It always protects, always trusts, always hopes, always perseveres. Love never fails.

1 CORINTHIANS 13:1–8

The fruit of the Spirit is love, joy, peace, patience, kindness, goodness, faithfulness.

GALATIANS 5:22

God did not give us a spirit of timidity, but a spirit of power, of love and of self-discipline.

2 TIMOTHY 1:7

There is no fear in love. But perfect love drives out fear.

1 JOHN 4:18

God so loved the world that he gave his one and only Son, that whoever believes in him shall not perish but have eternal life.

JOHN 3:16

This is how we know what love is: Jesus Christ laid down his life for us. And we ought to lay down our lives for our brothers.

1 JOHN 3:16

Love each other deeply, because love covers over a multitude of sins.

1 PETER 4:8

Keep yourselves in God's love as you wait for the mercy of our Lord Jesus Christ to bring you to eternal life.

JUDE 21

Mercy, peace and love be yours in abundance.

JUDE 2

We love because God first loved us.

1 JOHN 4:19

LOVE

LOVE LANGUAGES

June is the month of romance, but my husband's language of love doesn't include romantic walks under the moonlight, holding hands. Ken doesn't go for mushy sentiment. Watching a basketball game together is his idea of romance. But I'm not complaining. I've learned to appreciate his language of love.

I've also learned the Lord's language of love. When I tell Jesus that I love him, it has nothing to do with romance. But passion? Yes! My love for Jesus is not a syrupy sentiment, but it is definitely zealous and fervent, spirited and intense. When I praise him, I believe he deserves adoration filled with warmth and affection. When I sing to him, I want the melody to come right from my heart.

This is the language of love between God and his creation. We should love him this way because this is how he loves us. To love to the point of death is passion with a capital "P." This is the way we are to love our brothers and sisters.

Developing an artful language of love to the Lord will cost you something. It will cost you your pride and, most valued of all, your human logic. Throw your caution to the wind and invite the Spirit of God to fill your heart with the warmth and passion of praise.

JONI EARECKSON TADA

This is love: that we walk in obedience to his commands. As you have heard from the beginning, his command is that you walk in love.

2 JOHN 6

We will serve the LORD our God and obey him.

JOSHUA 24:24

"If you walk in my ways and obey my statutes and commands . . . I will give you a long life," says the LORD.

1 KINGS 3:14

This is how we know that we love the children of God: by loving God and carrying out his commands. This is love for God: to obey his commands. And his commands are not burdensome.

1 JOHN 5:2–3

From everlasting to everlasting the LORD's love is with those who fear him, and his righteousness with their children's children—with those who keep his covenant and remember to obey his precepts.

PSALM 103:17–18

Blessed are they who keep his statutes and seek him with all their heart. They do nothing wrong; they walk in his ways.

PSALM 119:2–3

❧

Jesus said, "Whoever has my commands and obeys them, he is the one who loves me. He who loves me will be loved by my Father, and I too will love him and show myself to him."

JOHN 14:21

I have kept my feet from every evil path so that I might obey your word, O LORD.

PSALM 119:101

Keeping God's commands is what counts.

1 CORINTHIANS 7:19

Obey me, and I will be your God and you will be my people. Walk in all the ways I command you, that it may go well with you.

JEREMIAH 7:23

We must obey God rather than men!

ACTS 5:29

Do not merely listen to the word, and so deceive yourselves. Do what it says. Anyone who listens to the word but does not do what it says is like a man who looks at his face in a mirror and, after looking at himself, goes away and immediately forgets what he looks like.

JAMES 1:22–24

God's Words of Life on
Obedience

You have declared this day that the Lord is your God and that you will walk in his ways, that you will keep his decrees, commands and laws, and that you will obey him.

Deuteronomy 26:17

To love him with all your heart, with all your understanding and with all your strength, and to love your neighbor as yourself is more important than all burnt offerings and sacrifices.

Mark 12:33

What does the Lord your God ask of you but to fear the Lord your God, to walk in all his ways, to love him, to serve the Lord your God with all your heart and with all your soul, and to observe the Lord's commands and decrees that I am giving you today for your own good?

Deuteronomy 10:12–13

I will always obey your law, for ever and ever.

Psalm 119:44

Keep my decrees and follow them. I am the Lord, who makes you holy.

Leviticus 20:8

THE BLESSING OF OBEDIENCE

How often in the course of a day, especially in summer, does the command "Shut the door!" ring out. We shut the door against the inroads of insects, pets, heat.

The woman in 2 Kings 4 had a two-fold need to shut her door. A creditor had come to take her two sons as slaves. She shut in her two boys. She shut out the world around them. A crisis called for nothing less than intervention from on high, and she had no intention of letting outside interests rob her of the answer to her fervent prayer. In her extreme need she gladly heeded the voice of Elisha, the man of God. The abundance of oil that God supplied met her need of paying debts.

We might well wonder what would have happened had she done everything else God commanded, but had left the door open. Distraction and possibly derision might have moved her to abandon the instructions given by the prophet. We can only speculate, but we do know that unless we deliberately shut out the world's noise there will be little chance to hear the voice of God.

JEANETTE LOCKERBIE

Everyone should be quick to listen, slow to speak and slow to become angry.

JAMES 1:19

It is good to wait quietly for the salvation of the LORD.

LAMENTATIONS 3:26

Wait for the LORD; be strong and take heart and wait for the LORD.

PSALM 27:14

Be joyful in hope, patient in affliction, faithful in prayer.

ROMANS 12:12

The testing of your faith develops perseverance. Perseverance must finish its work so that you may be mature and complete, not lacking anything.

JAMES 1:3–4

If we hope for what we do not yet have, we wait for it patiently.

ROMANS 8:25

You need to persevere so that when you have done the will of God, you will receive what he has promised.

HEBREWS 10:36

❦❧ ──────────────────

Be patient, then, brothers, until the Lord's coming. See how the farmer waits for the land to yield its valuable crop and how patient he is for the autumn and spring rains. You too, be patient and stand firm, because the Lord's coming is near.

JAMES 5:7–8

Let us not become weary in doing good, for at the proper time we will reap a harvest if we do not give up.

GALATIANS 6:9

Be completely humble and gentle; be patient, bearing with one another in love.

EPHESIANS 4:2

We pray this in order that you may live a life worthy of the Lord and may please him in every way: bearing fruit in every good work, growing in the knowledge of God, being strengthened with all power according to his glorious might so that you may have great endurance and patience.

COLOSSIANS 1:10–11

The fruit of the Spirit is love, joy, peace, patience, kindness, goodness, faithfulness, gentleness and self-control. Against such things there is no law.

GALATIANS 5:22–23

PATIENCE

You, O Lord, are a compassionate and gracious God, slow to anger, abounding in love and faithfulness.

PSALM 86:15

The LORD longs to be gracious to you; he rises to show you compassion. For the LORD is a God of justice. Blessed are all who wait for him!

ISAIAH 30:18

I was shown mercy so that in me, the worst of sinners, Christ Jesus might display his unlimited patience as an example for those who would believe on him and receive eternal life.

1 TIMOTHY 1:16

The Lord is not slow in keeping his promise, as some understand slowness. He is patient with you, not wanting anyone to perish, but everyone to come to repentance.

2 PETER 3:9

I waited patiently for the LORD;
    he turned to me and heard my cry.

PSALM 40:1

Patience is better than pride.

ECCLESIASTES 7:8

The seed on good soil stands for those with a noble and good heart, who hear the word, retain it, and by persevering produce a crop.

LUKE 8:15

[Love] always protects, always trusts, always hopes, always perseveres.

1 CORINTHIANS 13:7

We continually remember before our God and Father your work produced by faith, your labor prompted by love, and your endurance inspired by hope in our Lord Jesus Christ.

1 THESSALONIANS 1:3

Everything that was written in the past was written to teach us, so that through endurance and the encouragement of the Scriptures we might have hope. May the God who gives endurance and encouragement give you a spirit of unity among yourselves as you follow Christ Jesus.

ROMANS 15:4–5

As God's chosen people, holy and dearly loved, clothe yourselves with compassion, kindness, humility, gentleness and patience.

COLOSSIANS 3:12

Preach the Word; be prepared in season and out of season; correct, rebuke and encourage—with great patience and careful instruction.

2 TIMOTHY 4:2

Keep yourselves in God's love as you wait for the mercy of our Lord Jesus Christ to bring you to eternal life.

JUDE 21

I always thank God for you because of his grace given you in Christ Jesus. For in him you have been enriched in every way—in all your speaking and in all your knowledge ... Therefore you do not lack any spiritual gift as you eagerly wait for our Lord Jesus Christ to be revealed. He will keep you strong to the end, so that you will be blameless on the day of our Lord Jesus Christ. God, who has called you into fellowship with his Son Jesus Christ our Lord, is faithful.

1 CORINTHIANS 1:4–5,7–9

❧❦

THE PATIENCE OF JOB

You've heard of the patience of Job? To me that never made sense, because the book of Job is one long list of complaints. Job cried out in protest against God. Even his friends were shocked at his impudent anger. Most of us would bite our nails in fearful trembling if we ever talked to God that way.

God, however, does not get offended. In fact, in a supreme touch of irony, God orders Job's pious comforters to seek repentance from Job, the very source of so many heated complaints.

I love that about God. Where it concerned Job, the guy was only human. And, yes, his patience was gloriously played out in that he refused to curse God and die. But it was the Lord who demonstrated the very best of what it means to be patient. God, as it says elsewhere in Scripture, refused to break the bruised reed or snuff out the smoldering wick.

The patience of Job? I would think it should be the patience of God. The God of Job—your God—defends the hurting, uplifts the oppressed, and listens to the complaints of the suffering. He may not respond to your questions with neat, pat answers, but he will always, always answer your questions with his own patience.

JONI EARECKSON TADA

Jesus said, "Peace I leave with you; my peace I give you. I do not give to you as the world gives. Do not let your hearts be troubled and do not be afraid."

JOHN 14:27

LORD, you establish peace for us; all that we have accomplished you have done for us.

ISAIAH 26:12

Let the peace of Christ rule in your hearts, since as members of one body you were called to peace.

COLOSSIANS 3:15

The peace of God, which transcends all understanding, will guard your hearts and your minds in Christ Jesus.

PHILIPPIANS 4:7

I will lie down and sleep in peace, for you alone, O LORD, make me dwell in safety.

PSALM 4:8

The LORD gives strength to his people; the LORD blesses his people with peace.

PSALM 29:11

You will keep in perfect peace him whose mind is steadfast, because he trusts in you.

ISAIAH 26:3

The meek will inherit the land and enjoy great peace.

PSALM 37:11

Great peace have they who love your law, and nothing can make them stumble.

PSALM 119:165

Aim for perfection, listen to my appeal, be of one mind, live in peace. And the God of love and peace will be with you.

2 CORINTHIANS 13:11

Make every effort to keep the unity of the Spirit through the bond of peace.

EPHESIANS 4:3

The God of peace will be with you.

PHILIPPIANS 4:9

If it is possible, as far as it depends on you, live at peace with everyone.

ROMANS 12:18

The wisdom that comes from heaven is first of all pure; then peace-loving, considerate, submissive, full of mercy and good fruit, impartial and sincere. Peacemakers who sow in peace raise a harvest of righteousness.

JAMES 3:17–18

Blessed are the peacemakers, for they will be called sons of God.

MATTHEW 5:9

Submit to God and be at peace with him; in this way prosperity will come to you.

JOB 22:21

"Peace, peace, to those far and near," says the LORD. "And I will heal them."

ISAIAH 57:19

I will build you with stones of turquoise, your foundations with sapphires. I will make your battlements of rubies, your gates of sparkling jewels, and all your walls of precious stones. All your sons will be taught by the LORD, and great will be your children's peace. In righteousness you will be established.

ISAIAH 54:11–14

He will stand and shepherd his flock in the strength of the LORD, in the majesty of the name of the LORD his God. And they will live securely, for then his greatness will reach to the ends of the earth. And he will be their peace.

MICAH 5:4–5

Jesus said, "I have told you these things, so that in me you may have peace. In this world you will have trouble. But take heart! I have overcome the world."

JOHN 16:33

For to us a child is born, to us a son is given, and the government will be on his shoulders. And he will be called Wonderful Counselor, Mighty God, Everlasting Father, Prince of Peace.

ISAIAH 9:6

May the Lord of peace himself give you peace at all times and in every way.

2 THESSALONIANS 3:16

The fruit of righteousness will be peace; the effect of righteousness will be quietness and confidence forever.

ISAIAH 32:17

I the LORD will be their God . . . I will make a covenant of peace with them . . . I will bless them and the places surrounding my hill. I will send down showers in season; there will be showers of blessing.

EZEKIEL 34:24–26

I will listen to what God the LORD will say;
    he promises peace to his people, his saints.

PSALM 85:8

Seek peace and pursue it. For the eyes of the Lord are on the righteous and his ears are attentive to their prayer.

1 PETER 3:11–12

Pursue righteousness, faith, love and peace, along with those who call on the Lord out of a pure heart.

2 TIMOTHY 2:22

Mercy, peace and love be yours in abundance.

JUDE 2

Live in peace with each other.

1 THESSALONIANS 5:13

Jesus came and preached peace to you who were far away and peace to those who were near.

EPHESIANS 2:17

ᴅEVOTIONAL ᴛHOUGHT ON

PEACE

BLESSED ARE THE PEACEMAKERS

Last night Joe reminded me that it was time to start getting the income tax stuff together. I groaned, leaning back against the couch. "How I dread this time of year! Trying to find all the papers."

He raised an eyebrow and I knew what he was thinking. "You don't believe I have a system, do you?" I yelped.

"Hey! Did I say anything? All you have to do is dig out the records."

"But you just watch, some important paper will be missing. Like last year."

His eyebrow went up again. "You must have thrown it out. Like that gift certificate to the Velvet Turtle."

"The Velvet Turtle! You always bring that up." I could tell him about a few other things he'd mis-placed—like the whole garage. I started toward the kitchen, and unexpectedly, through Scripture, the Holy Spirit whispered: Blessed are the peacemakers.

I struggled with the Spirit a moment or two before I calmed down. I poured coffee and brought him a cup. "Honey, let's not argue. Things certainly do have a way of disappearing around here."

Alone in the bathroom, I thanked the Lord for clos-ing my mouth before I said anything else.

MAB GRAFF HOOVER

Jesus said, "This, then, is how you should pray: 'Our Father in heaven, hallowed be your name, your kingdom come, your will be done on earth as it is in heaven.'"

MATTHEW 6:9–10

We fix our eyes not on what is seen, but on what is unseen. For what is seen is temporary, but what is unseen is eternal.

2 CORINTHIANS 4:18

Whatever was to my profit I now consider loss for the sake of Christ.

PHILIPPIANS 3:7

Seek first God's kingdom and his righteousness, and all these things will be given to you as well.

MATTHEW 6:33

Since we are surrounded by such a great cloud of witnesses, let us throw off everything that hinders and the sin that so easily entangles, and let us run with perseverance the race marked out for us. Let us fix our eyes on Jesus, the author and perfecter of our faith, who for the joy set before him endured the cross, scorning its shame, and sat down at the right hand of the throne of God.

HEBREWS 12:1–2

By faith Moses, when he had grown up, refused to be known as the son of Pharaoh's daughter. He chose to be mistreated along with the people of God rather than to enjoy the pleasures of sin for a short time. He regarded disgrace for the sake of Christ as of greater value than the treasures of Egypt, because he was looking ahead to his reward.

HEBREWS 11:24–26

I consider my life worth nothing to me, if only I may finish the race and complete the task the Lord Jesus has given me—the task of testifying to the gospel of God's grace.

ACTS 20:24

Make my joy complete by being like-minded, having the same love, being one in spirit and purpose. Do nothing out of selfish ambition or vain conceit, but in humility consider others better than yourselves. Each of you should look not only to your own interests, but also to the interests of others. Your attitude should be the same as that of Christ Jesus.

PHILIPPIANS 2:2–5

In Christ Jesus neither circumcision nor uncircumcision has any value. The only thing that counts is faith expressing itself through love.

GALATIANS 5:6

Someone will say, "You have faith; I have deeds."
Show me your faith without deeds, and I will show
you my faith by what I do.

JAMES 2:18

Jesus said, "Not everyone who says to me, "Lord,
Lord," will enter the kingdom of heaven, but only he
who does the will of my Father who is in heaven."

MATTHEW 7:21

Let us not love with words or tongue but with
actions and in truth.

1 JOHN 3:18

Whatever you do, work at it with all your heart, as
working for the Lord, not for men, since you know
that you will receive an inheritance from the Lord
as a reward. It is the Lord Christ you are serving.

COLOSSIANS 3:23–24

When times are good, be happy; but when times
are bad, consider: God has made the one as well
as the other. Therefore, a man cannot discover
anything about his future.

ECCLESIASTES 7:14

Set your minds on things above, not on earthly
things.

COLOSSIANS 3:2

There is a time for everything, and a season for every activity under heaven: a time to be born and a time to die, a time to plant and a time to uproot, a time to kill and a time to heal, a time to tear down and a time to build, a time to weep and a time to laugh, a time to mourn and a time to dance, a time to scatter stones and a time to gather them, a time to embrace and a time to refrain, a time to search and a time to give up, a time to keep and a time to throw away, a time to tear and a time to mend, a time to be silent and a time to speak, a time to love and a time to hate, a time for war and a time for peace.

ECCLESIASTES 3:1–8

"My thoughts are not your thoughts, neither are your ways my ways," declares the LORD. "As the heavens are higher than the earth, so are my ways higher than your ways and my thoughts than your thoughts."

ISAIAH 55:8–9

Praise and exalt and glorify the King of heaven, because everything he does is right and all his ways are just.

DANIEL 4:37

The LORD does not look at the things man looks at. Man looks at the outward appearance, but the LORD looks at the heart.

1 SAMUEL 16:7

Jesus said, "I praise you, Father, Lord of heaven and earth, because you have hidden these things from the wise and learned, and revealed them to little children. Yes, Father, for this was your good pleasure."

MATTHEW 11:25–26

Oh, the depth of the riches of the wisdom and knowledge of God! How unsearchable his judgments, and his paths beyond tracing out! "Who has known the mind of the Lord? Or who has been his counselor?" "Who has ever given to God, that God should repay him?" For from him and through him and to him are all things. To him be the glory forever! Amen.

ROMANS 11:33–36

Your ways, O God, are holy. What god is so great as our God? You are the God who performs miracles; you display your power among the peoples.

PSALM 77:13–14

[Abel, Enoch, Noah, Abraham] . . . all these people were still living by faith when they died. They did not receive the things promised; they only saw them and welcomed them from a distance. And they admitted that they were aliens and strangers on earth. People who say such things show that they are looking for a country of their own. If they had been thinking of the country they had left, they would have had opportunity to return. Instead, they were longing for a better country—a heavenly one. Therefore God is not ashamed to be called their God, for he has prepared a city for them.

HEBREWS 11:13–16

Jesus said, "Look at the birds of the air; they do not sow or reap or store away in barns, and yet your heavenly Father feeds them. Are you not much more valuable than they? Who of you by worrying can add a single hour to his life? And why do you worry about clothes? See how the lilies of the field grow. They do not labor or spin. Yet I tell you that not even Solomon in all his splendor was dressed like one of these."

MATTHEW 6:26–29

The world and its desires pass away, but the [one] who does the will of God lives forever.

1 JOHN 2:17

Jesus said, "In my Father's house are many rooms;
if it were not so, I would have told you. I am
going there to prepare a place for you. And if I go
and prepare a place for you, I will come back and
take you to be with me that you also may be
where I am."

JOHN 14:2–3

God understands the way to wisdom and he alone
knows where it dwells, for he views the ends of
the earth and sees everything under the heavens.

JOB 28:23–24

Delight yourself in the LORD
    and he will give you the desires of your heart.
Commit your way to the LORD;
    trust in him and he will do this:
He will make your righteousness shine like the dawn,
    the justice of your cause like the noonday sun.

PSALM 37:4–6

Let us not become weary in doing good, for at the
proper time we will reap a harvest if we do not
give up.

GALATIANS 6:9

❧

AN UNHURRIED PERSPECTIVE

I remember when we rode along country roads in a Model T Ford—back when people were not in such a hurry. The roads were not the current-day straight, smooth ribbons of concrete. And the cars wouldn't travel as fast as our modern ones do. We had time to stop for cattails when dad took us on Sunday-afternoon drives. We enjoyed the scenery, slow motion. We took time to pick wild berries and flowers along the way. I loved it!

If it's a sign of old age to admit to a longing for a slower pace, then I am getting old. Too often we get to our destination and wonder if it was worth the trouble. We don't spend even our leisure time "leisurely" anymore!

I need to slow down. And I'm asking the Lord to help me do it. I want to move slowly enough to be aware of all the joys he has hidden for me. I want to slow down enough to grow as he wants me to grow. I want to be quiet enough to hear his voice. I need his wisdom to know how to spend my time and how to order my days.

KATHRYN HILLEN

GOD'S WORDS OF LIFE ON
PRAYER

"Before they call I will answer; while they are still speaking I will hear," says the LORD.

ISAIAH 65:24

Whatever you ask for in prayer, believe that you have received it, and it will be yours.

MARK 11:24

Ask and it will be given to you; seek and you will find; knock and the door will be opened to you. For everyone who asks receives; he who seeks finds; and to him who knocks, the door will be opened.

MATTHEW 7:7–8

Jesus said, "I tell you that if two of you on earth agree about anything you ask for, it will be done for you by my Father in heaven. For where two or three come together in my name, there am I with them."

MATTHEW 18:19–20

Dear friends, if our hearts do not condemn us, we have confidence before God and receive from him anything we ask, because we obey his commands and do what pleases him.

1 JOHN 3:21–22

When you pray, go into your room, close the door and pray to your Father, who is unseen. Then your Father, who sees what is done in secret, will reward you.

MATTHEW 6:6

The LORD is near to all who call on him, to all who call on him in truth.

PSALM 145:18

"Call to me and I will answer you and tell you great and unsearchable things you do not know," says the LORD.

JEREMIAH 33:3

"He will call upon me, and I will answer him; I will be with him in trouble, I will deliver him and honor him," declares the LORD.

PSALM 91:15

The LORD is far from the wicked but he hears the prayer of the righteous.

PROVERBS 15:29

Delight yourself in the LORD and he will give you the desires of your heart.

PSALM 37:4

Let us then approach the throne of grace with confidence, so that we may receive mercy and find grace to help us in our time of need.

HEBREWS 4:16

Jesus said, "I tell you the truth, my Father will give you whatever you ask in my name. Until now you have not asked for anything in my name. Ask and you will receive, and your joy will be complete."

JOHN 16:23–24

If we confess our sins, God is faithful and just and will forgive us our sins and purify us from all unrighteousness.

1 JOHN 1:9

Jesus said, "I will do whatever you ask in my name, so that the Son may bring glory to the Father. You may ask me for anything in my name, and I will do it."

JOHN 14:13–14

"If my people, who are called by my name, will humble themselves and pray and seek my face and turn from their wicked ways, then will I hear from heaven and will forgive their sin and will heal their land," declares the LORD.

2 CHRONICLES 7:14

GOD'S WORDS OF LIFE ON
PRAYER

I wait for you, O LORD; you will answer, O LORD my God.

PSALM 38:15

If you believe, you will receive whatever you ask for in prayer.

MATTHEW 21:22

Jesus said, "If you remain in me and my words remain in you, ask whatever you wish, and it will be given you."

JOHN 15:7

Very early in the morning, while it was still dark, Jesus got up, left the house and went off to a solitary place, where he prayed.

MARK 1:35

Is any one of you in trouble? He should pray. Is anyone happy? Let him sing songs of praise. Is any one of you sick? He should call the elders of the church to pray over him and anoint him with oil in the name of the Lord. And the prayer offered in faith will make the sick person well; the Lord will raise him up. If he has sinned, he will be forgiven. Therefore confess your sins to each other and pray for each other so that you may be healed.

JAMES 5:13–16

This is the confidence we have in approaching God: that if we ask anything according to his will, he hears us. And if we know that he hears us—whatever we ask—we know that we have what we asked of him.

1 JOHN 5:14–15

The eyes of the Lord are on the righteous and his ears are attentive to their prayer.

1 PETER 3:12

Dear friends, build yourselves up in your most holy faith and pray in the Holy Spirit.

JUDE 20

Everything God created is good, and nothing is to be rejected if it is received with thanksgiving, because it is consecrated by the word of God and prayer.

1 TIMOTHY 4:4–5

I urge, first of all, that requests, prayers, intercession and thanksgiving be made for everyone—for kings and all those in authority, that we may live peaceful and quiet lives in all godliness and holiness.

1 TIMOTHY 2:1–2

❧❧

PRAY WITHOUT CEASING

God emphasizes the importance of prayer. Needs are supplied, problems solved, the impossible accomplished through prayer. Therefore we ought to pray. We may not feel like it, but we ought to pray. We may be discouraged, but we ought to pray.

We are always to pray—not merely when we have a need or only at some set time, but always. The line to heaven is always open. We are sometimes prone to make our own plans or decisions before we pray, but we should pray about everything first.

Not only are we to pray, but we are not to faint. Perhaps we have been praying about something for a long time and do not see the answer. We may think God hasn't heard or doesn't care. However, we are not to faint. I once witnessed the joy of one who had just received word that her brother had become a Christian. With tears running down her cheeks, she said, as she related her inspiring experience, "I have prayed for him for forty years." Rubinstein, the famous composer and pianist, once said, "If I fail to practice one day, I notice it; if two days, my friends notice it; if three days, my public notices it."

MILLIE STAMM

A friend loves at all times, and a brother is born for adversity.

PROVERBS 17:17

My intercessor is my friend as my eyes pour out tears to God.

JOB 16:20

He who covers over an offense promotes love, but whoever repeats the matter separates close friends.

PROVERBS 17:9

Many companions may come to ruin, but there is a friend who sticks closer than a brother.

PROVERBS 18:24

Wounds from a friend can be trusted, but an enemy multiplies kisses.

PROVERBS 27:6

Jesus said, "Greater love has no one than this, that he lay down his life for his friends. You are my friends if you do what I command."

JOHN 15:13–14

The pleasantness of one's friend springs from his earnest counsel.

PROVERBS 27:9

Two are better than one, because they have a good return for their work: If one falls down, his friend can help him up. But pity the [one] who falls and has no one to help him up!

ECCLESIASTES 4:9–10

Bear with each other and forgive whatever grievances you may have against one another. Forgive as the Lord forgave you.

COLOSSIANS 3:13

By the grace given me I say to every one of you: Do not think of yourself more highly than you ought, but rather think of yourself with sober judgment, in accordance with the measure of faith God has given you. Just as each of us has one body with many members, and these members do not all have the same function, so in Christ we who are many form one body, and each member belongs to all the others.

ROMANS 12:3–5

Be completely humble and gentle; be patient, bearing with one another in love. Make every effort to keep the unity of the Spirit through the bond of peace.

EPHESIANS 4:2–3

RELATIONSHIPS

As believers in our glorious Lord Jesus Christ, don't show favoritism.

JAMES 2:1

Jesus said, "See that you do not look down on one of these little ones. For I tell you that their angels in heaven always see the face of my Father in heaven."

MATTHEW 18:10

Do not rebuke an older man harshly, but exhort him as if he were your father. Treat younger men as brothers, older women as mothers, and younger women as sisters, with absolute purity.

1 TIMOTHY 5:1–2

Carry each other's burdens, and in this way you will fulfill the law of Christ.

GALATIANS 6:2

Love one another deeply, from the heart.

1 PETER 1:22

Agree with one another so that there may be no divisions among you and that you may be perfectly united in mind and thought.

1 CORINTHIANS 1:10

Whoever loves God must also love his brother.

1 JOHN 4:21

Train a child in the way he should go, and when he is old he will not turn from it.

PROVERBS 22:6

Be careful, and watch yourselves closely so that you do not forget the things your eyes have seen or let them slip from your heart as long as you live. Teach them to your children and to their children after them.

DEUTERONOMY 4:9

I prayed for this child, and the LORD has granted me what I asked of him. So now I give him to the LORD. For his whole life he will be given over to the LORD.

1 SAMUEL 1:27-28

Children, obey your parents in the Lord, for this is right. "Honor your father and mother"—which is the first commandment with a promise—"that it may go well with you and that you may enjoy long life on the earth."

EPHESIANS 6:1-3

A man will leave his father and mother and be united to his wife, and the two will become one flesh.

EPHESIANS 5:31

If we walk in the light, as he is in the light, we have fellowship with one another.

1 JOHN 1:7

Respect those who work hard among you, who are over you in the Lord and who admonish you. Hold them in the highest regard in love because of their work.

1 THESSALONIANS 5:12–13

If you are offering your gift at the altar and there remember that your brother has something against you, leave your gift there in front of the altar. First go and be reconciled to your brother; then come and offer your gift.

MATTHEW 5:23–24

Dear children, let us not love with words or tongue but with actions and in truth.

1 JOHN 3:17–18

As we have opportunity, let us do good to all people, especially to those who belong to the family of believers.

GALATIANS 6:10

❧

GOD'S FRIENDS

How do you like your friends? Do you like them to be faithful and loyal? Encouraging, thoughtful, and kind? But how many of your friends would measure up to such standards?

Friends are people, and people are not always faithful and kind. Just look at some of the people Jesus called his friends. Peter was always interrupting and telling Jesus what he should do. Then there was Mary Magdalene, whose sordid past was well known. Indecisive Thomas never stood up for his opinions. Then there was Nicodemus, a chicken for not showing his face in the daytime.

These people had their problems. Nevertheless, Jesus valued them as friends. He didn't expect them to be perfect; he expected them to be themselves, faults and fine points together. And all he asked of them was their love. Love for him and for each other.

Perhaps you're the type who forgets appointments or birthdays. Housecleaning doesn't top your priority list. You get intimidated easily and fail to stick up for your friends. Aren't you glad that none of these things disqualify you from your Lord's circle of friends?

Jesus says that you are his friend if you do two things: Love God and love others.

JONI EARECKSON TADA

Jesus said, "Come to me, all you who are weary and burdened, and I will give you rest. Take my yoke upon you and learn from me, for I am gentle and humble in heart, and you will find rest for your souls. For my yoke is easy and my burden is light."

MATTHEW 11:28–30

God gives strength to the weary and increases the power of the weak. Even youths grow tired and weary, and young men stumble and fall; but those who hope in the LORD will renew their strength. They will soar on wings like eagles; they will run and not grow weary, they will walk and not be faint.

ISAIAH 40:29–31

"I will refresh the weary and satisfy the faint," says the LORD.

JEREMIAH 31:25

The LORD makes me lie down in green pastures, he leads me beside quiet waters, he restores my soul. He guides me in paths of righteousness for his name's sake.

PSALM 23:2–3

Since the promise of entering God's rest still stands, let us be careful that none of you be found to have fallen short of it.

HEBREWS 4:1

The apostles gathered around Jesus and reported to him all they had done and taught. Then, because so many people were coming and going that they did not even have a chance to eat, he said to them, "Come with me by yourselves to a quiet place and get some rest."

MARK 6:30–31

Find rest, O my soul, in God alone;
my hope comes from him.

PSALM 62:5

Restore us, O God; make your face shine upon us.

PSALM 80:3

The LORD replied, "My Presence will go with you, and I will give you rest."

EXODUS 33:14

Let the beloved of the LORD rest secure in him, for he shields him all day long, and the one the LORD loves rests between his shoulders.

DEUTERONOMY 33:12

He who dwells in the shelter of the Most High will rest in the shadow of the Almighty.

PSALM 91:1

God's Words of Life on
Rest

This is what the LORD says: "Stand at the cross-roads and look; ask for the ancient paths, ask where the good way is, and walk in it, and you will find rest for your souls."

JEREMIAH 6:16

God will speak to this people . . . "This is the resting place, let the weary rest," and, "This is the place of repose."

ISAIAH 28:11–12

Be at rest once more, O my soul, for the LORD has been good to you.

PSALM 116:7

The LORD is with you when you are with him. If you seek him, he will be found by you.

2 CHRONICLES 15:2

The eternal God is your refuge, and underneath are the everlasting arms.

DEUTERONOMY 33:27

❧

IN REST, FIND GOD

In the solitude of a cave Elijah experienced God's awesome healing and saving power. The Lord had allowed Elijah to rest for a moment before reminding him that he understood and knew his pain.

Elijah came out of the cave and found that the Lord was an ever-present reality. Elijah was not alone! The earthquake and the fire both got his attention. Yet, it was in the still, small voice—a whisper from God— that Elijah rediscovered the Lord for himself.

Perhaps out of Elijah's experience we can find hope and help for our own lives. God made a time and place for Elijah to pull away from his ministry to rest. In the same way, God allows us to retreat and rest from our weariness and fears. He gives us this time to allow ourselves to relax physically, spiritually, and mentally so that we can recognize the presence of God.

We often feel alone because God does not manifest himself in our lives with great fanfare but in quiet, barely perceptible ways. Perhaps we can learn to be still and sit silently so we can recognize the presence of God. As the psalmist said, "Be still, and know that I am God" (Psalm 46:10). For the Lord is always faithful to his Word, saying, "Never will I leave you; never will I forsake you" (Hebrews 13:5).

REVEREND DR. CHERYL CLEMETSON

SELF-IMAGE

Then God said, "Let us make man in our image, in our likeness..." So God created man in his own image, in the image of God he created him; male and female he created them.

GENESIS 1:26–27

You, O LORD, created my inmost being; you knit me together in my mother's womb. I praise you because I am fearfully and wonderfully made; your works are wonderful, I know that full well.

PSALM 139:13–14

Do you not know that your body is a temple of the Holy Spirit, who is in you, whom you have received from God? You are not your own; you were bought at a price. Therefore honor God with your body.

1 CORINTHIANS 6:19–20

We are God's workmanship, created in Christ Jesus to do good works, which God prepared in advance for us to do.

EPHESIANS 2:10

"I know the plans I have for you," declares the LORD, "plans to prosper you and not to harm you, plans to give you hope and a future."

JEREMIAH 29:11

You were taught, with regard to your former way of life, to put off your old self, which is being corrupted by its deceitful desires; to be made new in the attitude of your minds; and to put on the new self, created to be like God in true righteousness and holiness.

EPHESIANS 4:22–24

Jesus said, "Are not two sparrows sold for a penny? Yet not one of them will fall to the ground apart from the will of your Father. And even the very hairs of your head are all numbered. So don't be afraid; you are worth more than many sparrows."

MATTHEW 10:29–31

The Spirit himself testifies with our spirit that we are God's children. Now if we are children, then we are heirs—heirs of God and co-heirs with Christ, if indeed we share in his sufferings in order that we may also share in his glory.

ROMANS 8:16–17

How great is the love the Father has lavished on us, that we should be called children of God! And that is what we are!

1 JOHN 3:1

GOD'S WORDS OF LIFE ON
SELF-IMAGE

God chose us in him before the creation of the world to be holy and blameless in his sight. In love he predestined us to be adopted as his sons through Jesus Christ, in accordance with his pleasure and will—to the praise of his glorious grace, which he has freely given us in the One he loves.

EPHESIANS 1:4–6

God has reconciled you by Christ's physical body through death to present you holy in his sight, without blemish and free from accusation.

COLOSSIANS 1:22

You were washed, you were sanctified, you were justified in the name of the Lord Jesus Christ and by the Spirit of our God.

1 CORINTHIANS 6:11

You have been given fullness in Christ, who is the head over every power and authority.

COLOSSIANS 2:10

We are therefore Christ's ambassadors, as though God were making his appeal through us.

2 CORINTHIANS 5:20

ANOREXIC FAITH

I was struggling with anorexia nervosa. I had been obsessed with everything about my physical appearance. God tells me that the condition of my heart is important to him, much more important than the condition of my body. I had placed my hope, not in God's unconditional love, but in controlling my weight.

When I sank below eighty pounds, my internal battle intensified. I was a Christian, desiring to serve God, yet enslaved to food. I was miserable. Night after night I sobbed into my pillow, pleading that God would make me normal.

He answered those prayers slowly and gently. First, he showed me my sin and forgave me. He gave me caring friends to talk to, reassurance from his Word, and a wonderful husband. Michael loves me, not my dress size!

And, as confirmation that my healing is complete, God has given us three beautiful children—our three miracles, we call them, since I was told I would never be able to bear children as a result of my anorexia.

Now I desire only to fear God and put my hope in his love . . . and through his strength, I will delight only in him!

DEBBIE SMITH

SERVING

Your attitude should be the same as that of Christ Jesus: Who, being in very nature God, did not consider equality with God something to be grasped, but made himself nothing, taking the very nature of a servant, being made in human likeness. And being found in appearance as a man, he humbled himself and became obedient to death—even death on a cross!

PHILIPPIANS 2:5–8

Jesus said, "The greatest among you should be like the youngest, and the one who rules like the one who serves. For who is greater, the one who is at the table or the one who serves? Is it not the one who is at the table? But I am among you as one who serves."

LUKE 22:26–27

Though I am free and belong to no man, I make myself a slave to everyone, to win as many as possible. I have become all things to all men so that by all possible means I might save some.

1 CORINTHIANS 9:19, 22

There are different kinds of service, but the same Lord.

1 CORINTHIANS 12:5

❧❧

Jesus said, "For whoever wants to save his life will lose it, but whoever loses his life for me will find it."

MATTHEW 16:25

It is the LORD your God you must follow, and him you must revere. Keep his commands and obey him; serve him and hold fast to him.

DEUTERONOMY 13:4

Jesus said, "I have set you an example that you should do as I have done for you. I tell you the truth, no servant is greater than his master, nor is a messenger greater than the one who sent him."

JOHN 13:15–16

If serving the LORD seems undesirable to you, then choose for yourselves this day whom you will serve . . . But as for me and my household, we will serve the LORD.

JOSHUA 24:15

Be sure to fear the LORD and serve him faithfully with all your heart; consider what great things he has done for you.

1 SAMUEL 12:24

If anyone serves, he should do it with the strength God provides, so that in all things God may be praised through Jesus Christ.

1 PETER 4:11

Do not use your freedom to indulge the sinful nature; rather, serve one another in love.

GALATIANS 5:13

Each one should use whatever gift he has received to serve others, faithfully administering God's grace in its various forms.

1 PETER 4:10

Those who have served well gain an excellent standing and great assurance in their faith in Christ Jesus.

1 TIMOTHY 3:13

I thank Christ Jesus our Lord, who has given me strength, that he considered me faithful, appointing me to his service.

1 TIMOTHY 1:12

SERVING A WORTHY MASTER

B eing a servant is one of the most important lessons for Christians to learn; but unfortunately,
we often have to work through gross misconcep-
tions. We have fears about entrusting ourselves to
any boss, but we must learn in our spiritual journey
that this Master is unlike any other. He will not
abuse us or misuse us. He has our greatest interest
at heart. He encourages us through our servanthood
to be all that we can be and then gives us his own
Holy Spirit to empower us to become so. This
Master is one who even laid down his life for those
who were his servants.

He is a Master unlike any other. Not to be feared, he
is worthy of our service.

Many of us think servanthood means losing ourselves in such a way that we become people without
personality, people without original thinking ability,
people without giftedness. But when one serves this
Master, the opposite is true: He makes us full, complete human beings filled with his own image, with
his own amazing mentality. Paradoxically, while
teaching us to be more like him, we become more of
whom he created us to be.

KAREN BURTON MAINS

Jesus said, "Whoever finds his life will lose it, and whoever loses his life for my sake will find it."

MATTHEW 10:39

Whoever lives by the truth comes into the light, so that it may be seen plainly that what he has done has been done through God.

JOHN 3:21

Jesus said, "Remain in me, and I will remain in you. No branch can bear fruit by itself; it must remain in the vine. Neither can you bear fruit unless you remain in me. I am the vine; you are the branches . . . apart from me you can do nothing."

JOHN 15:4–5

Those who live according to the sinful nature have their minds set on what that nature desires; but those who live in accordance with the Spirit have their minds set on what the Spirit desires.

ROMANS 8:5

What does the LORD require of you? To act justly and to love mercy and to walk humbly with your God.

MICAH 6:8

Jesus said, "In the same way, any of you who does not give up everything he has cannot be my disciple."

LUKE 14:33

Jesus said, "By this all men will know that you are my disciples, if you love one another."

JOHN 13:35

Jesus replied, "If anyone loves me, he will obey my teaching. My Father will love him, and we will come to him and make our home with him."

JOHN 14:23

The grace of God that brings salvation has appeared to all men. It teaches us to say "No" to ungodliness and worldly passions, and to live self-controlled, upright and godly lives in this present age.

TITUS 2:11–12

Jesus said, "Everyone who hears these words of mine and puts them into practice is like a wise man who built his house on the rock. The rain came down, the streams rose, and the winds blew and beat against that house; yet it did not fall, because it had its foundation on the rock. But everyone who hears these words of mine and does not put them into practice is like a foolish man who built his house on sand. The rain came down, the streams rose, and the winds blew and beat against that house, and it fell with a great crash."

MATTHEW 7:24–27

Forgetting what is behind and straining toward what is ahead, I press on toward the goal to win the prize for which God has called me heavenward in Christ Jesus.

PHILIPPIANS 3:13–14

Jesus said, "Whoever believes in me, as the Scripture has said, streams of living water will flow from within him."

JOHN 7:38

Grow in the grace and knowledge of our Lord and Savior Jesus Christ. To him be glory both now and forever!

2 PETER 3:18

Make every effort to add to your faith goodness; and to goodness, knowledge; and to knowledge, self-control; and to self-control, perseverance; and to perseverance, godliness; and to godliness, brotherly kindness; and to brotherly kindness, love. For if you possess these qualities in increasing measure, they will keep you from being ineffective and unproductive in your knowledge of our Lord Jesus Christ.

2 PETER 1:6–8

SPIRITUAL LIFE

THE RIVER OF THE HOLY SPIRIT

Jesus said, "Whoever believes in me . . . streams of living water will flow from within him" (John 7:38). This refers not to water but to the Holy Spirit who, when turned loose in our lives, strengthens, grows, and gives us vibrancy. As we allow the Holy Spirit to proceed from God and grow stronger, deeper, wider, and more pervasive, our spiritual and physical person takes on new, eternal, and abundant life. Only as we allow the Holy Spirit to flow in our thoughts, emotions, will, desires, dispositions, actions and activities does spiritual transformation take place. Then people can look at us in the midst of tribulation and say, "I think I see the Son of God." Our captors can look in the fiery furnaces and see us walk in confidence as we are accompanied by the fourth man.

I want God's waters to flow deeply and widely and expansively throughout this being of mine. I want the river of the Holy Spirit to so fill and guide me that I become a remote temple from which a branch of God's river can flow. I pray that God will let the waters flow in me, as I pray you will ask God to let his waters flow in you.

REVEREND DR. ALICIA D. BYRD

Just as the sufferings of Christ flow over into our lives, so also through Christ our comfort overflows.

2 CORINTHIANS 1:5

It has been granted to you on behalf of Christ not only to believe on him, but also to suffer for him.

PHILIPPIANS 1:29

[The Messiah] was despised and rejected by men, a man of sorrows, and familiar with suffering. Like one from whom men hide their faces he was despised, and we esteemed him not.

ISAIAH 53:3

Our present sufferings are not worth comparing with the glory that will be revealed in us.

ROMANS 8:18

For Christ's sake, I delight in weaknesses, in insults, in hardships, in persecutions, in difficulties. For when I am weak, then I am strong.

2 CORINTHIANS 12:10

Cast your cares on the LORD and he will sustain you; he will never let the righteous fall.

PSALM 55:22

He knows the way that I take; when he has tested me, I will come forth as gold.

JOB 23:10

The LORD disciplines those he loves.

PROVERBS 3:12

If you are insulted because of the name of Christ, you are blessed, for the Spirit of glory and of God rests on you.

1 PETER 4:14

Everyone who wants to live a godly life in Christ Jesus will be persecuted.

2 TIMOTHY 3:12

Do not despise the discipline of the Almighty. For he wounds, but he also binds up; he injures, but his hands also heal.

JOB 5:17-18

We also rejoice in our sufferings, because we know that suffering produces perseverance; perseverance, character; and character, hope.

ROMANS 5:3-4

No discipline seems pleasant at the time, but painful. Later on, however, it produces a harvest of righteousness and peace for those who have been trained by it.

HEBREWS 12:11

Consider it pure joy . . . whenever you face trials of many kinds, because you know that the testing of your faith develops perseverance.

JAMES 1:2-3

God has not despised or disdained the suffering of the afflicted one; he has not hidden his face from him but has listened to his cry for help.

PSALM 22:24

Those who sow in tears will reap with songs of joy. He who goes out weeping, carrying seed to sow, will return with songs of joy, carrying sheaves with him.

PSALM 126:5-6

STRUGGLES

🙖〰

SHINING IN DARK TIMES

Esther must have wondered so often about the plan of God and his promises. The plan of God was to redeem lost mankind. That divine plan concerned her nation Israel. From this special people, the bright Morning Star, the Messiah himself, would come. Esther literally staked her life on these bright and enduring promises, and she trusted even when she lived in possibly one of the blackest and darkest periods of her nation's history.

This we know, she staked her life on the providence of God that would enable him to keep his promises concerning his plan.

What happens to us when we find ourselves in the middle of dark situations? Do we believe the things that are happening to us are accidental? Do we seek to change our circumstances, or do we accept them with a fatalistic attitude? Can we change our circumstances, or should we even try?

Sometimes we can change things, and we must try. That is why we are there! At other times, having tried, we find we cannot alter anything, nor can we escape, and so we must allow those situations to change us and we must accept the privilege of shining there.

JILL BRISCOE

169

There are different kinds of gifts, but the same Spirit. There are different kinds of service, but the same Lord. There are different kinds of working, but the same God works all of them in all men. Now to each one the manifestation of the Spirit is given for the common good. To one there is given through the Spirit the message of wisdom, to another the message of knowledge by means of the same Spirit, to another faith by the same Spirit, to another gifts of healing by that one Spirit, to another miraculous powers, to another prophecy, to another distinguishing between spirits, to another speaking in different kinds of tongues, and to still another the interpretation of tongues. All these are the work of one and the same Spirit, and he gives them to each one, just as he determines.

1 CORINTHIANS 12:4–11

To one he gave five talents of money, to another two talents, and to another one talent, each according to his ability. Then he went on his journey. The man who had received the five talents went at once and put his money to work and gained five more. So also, the one with the two talents gained two more. But the man who had received the one talent went off, dug a hole in the ground and hid his master's money.

After a long time the master of those servants returned and settled accounts with them. The man who had received the five talents brought the other five. "Master," he said, "you entrusted me with five talents. See, I have gained five more." His master replied, "Well done, good and faithful servant! You have been faithful with a few things; I will put you in charge of many things. Come and share your master's happiness!" The man with the two talents also came. "Master," he said, "you entrusted me with two talents; see, I have gained two more." His master replied, "Well done, good and faithful servant! You have been faithful with a few things; I will put you in charge of many things. Come and share your master's happiness!" Then the man who had received the one talent came. "Master," he said, "I knew that you are a hard man, harvesting where you have not sown and gathering where you have not scattered seed. So I was afraid and went out and hid your talent in the ground. See, here is what belongs to you." His master replied, "You wicked, lazy servant! So you knew that I harvest where I have not sown and gather where I have not scattered seed? Well then, you should have put my money on deposit with the bankers, so that when I returned I would have received it back with interest. Take the talent from him and give it to the one who has the ten talents. For everyone who has will be given more, and he will have an abundance."

MATTHEW 25:15–29

Remember the LORD your God, for it is he who gives you the ability to produce wealth.

DEUTERONOMY 8:18

In everything set them an example by doing what is good. In your teaching show integrity, seriousness and soundness of speech that cannot be condemned.

TITUS 2:7–8

May he give you the desire of your heart
and make all your plans succeed.

PSALM 20:4

I remind you to fan into flame the gift of God, which is in you.

2 TIMOTHY 1:6

In the church God has appointed first of all apostles, second prophets, third teachers, then workers of miracles, also those having gifts of healing, those able to help others, those with gifts of administration, and those speaking in different kinds of tongues. Are all apostles? Are all prophets? Are all teachers? Do all work miracles? Do all have gifts of healing? Do all speak in tongues? Do all interpret? But eagerly desire the greater gifts.

1 CORINTHIANS 12:28–31

Every good and perfect gift is from above, coming down from the Father of the heavenly lights, who does not change like shifting shadows.

JAMES 1:17

You do not lack any spiritual gift as you eagerly wait for our Lord Jesus Christ to be revealed.

1 CORINTHIANS 1:7

Each one should use whatever gift he has received to serve others, faithfully administering God's grace in its various forms. If anyone speaks, he should do it as one speaking the very words of God. If anyone serves, he should do it with the strength God provides, so that in all things God may be praised through Jesus Christ.

1 PETER 4:10–11

This salvation, which was first announced by the Lord, was confirmed to us by those who heard him. God also testified to it by signs, wonders and various miracles, and gifts of the Holy Spirit distributed according to his will.

HEBREWS 2:3–4

Since you are eager to have spiritual gifts, try to excel in gifts that build up the church.

1 CORINTHIANS 14:12

Each man has his own gift from God; one has this gift, another has that.

1 CORINTHIANS 7:7

Set an example for the believers in speech, in life, in love, in faith and in purity. Devote yourself to the public reading of Scripture, to preaching and to teaching. Do not neglect your gift, which was given you.

1 TIMOTHY 4:12–14

We have different gifts, according to the grace given us. If a man's gift is prophesying, let him use it in proportion to his faith. If it is serving, let him serve; if it is teaching, let him teach; if it is encouraging, let him encourage; if it is contributing to the needs of others, let him give generously; if it is leadership, let him govern diligently; if it is showing mercy, let him do it cheerfully.

ROMANS 12:6–8

God's Tools

There is a story told about a house which was badly in need of paint. "I am going to paint the house," said a can of paint, waiting, already mixed, in a shed. "No, I am going to paint it," the brush asserted, bristling with impatience. "You are, are you?" sneered the ladder, lying against the wall. "How far would either of you go without me?" "Or without me to pay the bill?" arrogantly added the checkbook belonging to the owner of the house, in a voice muffled by the pocket of the coat hanging on a nail. Just then the painter, who had overheard the proud remarks, ventured to put in a word. "Perhaps I'd better take a holiday," he said quietly. "I wonder if the house would be painted by the time I got back."

Even the most efficient among us are only tools in the hands of the Great Master Worker. As we work with him and for him, he works in us and through us. One worker is not more valuable or important than another. He that plants and he that waters have a unity of purpose. There is no reason for rivalry. Each has his task; each has his place. Perhaps it is our task to plant—or it may be to water. There may be times when we plant and other times when we water. But whatever our place may be, we are laboring with and for God. Then God will give the increase.

Millie Stamm

All of us also lived among them at one time, gratifying the cravings of our sinful nature and following its desires and thoughts. Like the rest, we were by nature objects of wrath. But because of his great love for us, God, who is rich in mercy, made us alive with Christ even when we were dead in transgressions—it is by grace you have been saved.

EPHESIANS 2:3-5

All have sinned and fall short of the glory of God.

ROMANS 3:23

The Scripture declares that the whole world is a prisoner of sin, so that what was promised, being given through faith in Jesus Christ, might be given to those who believe.

GALATIANS 3:22

If we confess our sins, he is faithful and just and will forgive us our sins and purify us from all unrighteousness.

1 JOHN 1:9

Your sins have been forgiven on account of his name.

1 JOHN 2:12

We all, like sheep, have gone astray, each of us has turned to his own way; and the LORD has laid on him the iniquity of us all.

ISAIAH 53:6

I acknowledged my sin to you
    and did not cover up my iniquity.
I said, "I will confess
    my transgressions to the LORD"—
and you forgave
    the guilt of my sin.

PSALM 32:5

He who conceals his sins does not prosper, but whoever confesses and renounces them finds mercy.

PROVERBS 28:13

God . . . commands all people everywhere to repent.

ACTS 17:30

God is faithful; he will not let you be tempted beyond what you can bear. But when you are tempted, he will also provide a way out so that you can stand up under it.

1 CORINTHIANS 10:13

Forgive us our sins, for we also forgive everyone who sins against us. And lead us not into temptation.

LUKE 11:4

Our struggle is not against flesh and blood, but against the rulers, against the authorities, against the powers of this dark world and against the spiritual forces of evil in the heavenly realms.

EPHESIANS 6:12

The Lord will rescue me from every evil attack and will bring me safely to his heavenly kingdom. To him be glory for ever and ever.

2 TIMOTHY 4:18

Watch and pray so that you will not fall into temptation. The spirit is willing, but the body is weak.

MATTHEW 26:41

Because Jesus himself suffered when he was tempted, he is able to help those who are being tempted.

HEBREWS 2:18

We know that our old self was crucified with Christ so that the body of sin might be done away with, that we should no longer be slaves to sin—because anyone who has died has been freed from sin.

ROMANS 6:6-7

For the wages of sin is death, but the gift of God is eternal life in Christ Jesus our Lord.

ROMANS 6:23

Since Christ was raised from the dead, he cannot die again; death no longer has mastery over him. The death he died, he died to sin once for all; but the life he lives, he lives to God. In the same way, count yourselves dead to sin but alive to God in Christ Jesus.

ROMANS 6:9-11

There is now no condemnation for those who are in Christ Jesus, because through Christ Jesus the law of the Spirit of life set me free from the law of sin and death.

ROMANS 8:1-2

If we walk in the light, as he is in the light, we have fellowship with one another, and the blood of Jesus, his Son, purifies us from all sin.

1 JOHN 1:7

Do not be deceived: God cannot be mocked. A man reaps what he sows. The one who sows to please his sinful nature, from that nature will reap destruction; the one who sows to please the Spirit, from the Spirit will reap eternal life.

GALATIANS 6:7-8

TEMPTATION

Confess your sins to each other and pray for each other.

JAMES 5:16

For we do not have a high priest who is unable to sympathize with our weaknesses, but we have one who has been tempted in every way, just as we are—yet was without sin. Let us then approach the throne of grace with confidence, so that we may receive mercy and find grace to help us in our time of need.

HEBREWS 4:15–16

It is for freedom that Christ has set us free. Stand firm, then, and do not let yourselves be burdened again by a yoke of slavery.

GALATIANS 5:1

Everyone who sins breaks the law; in fact, sin is lawlessness. But you know that Jesus appeared so that he might take away our sins. And in him is no sin.

1 JOHN 3:4–5

When you were dead in your sins . . . God made you alive with Christ. He forgave us all our sins, having canceled the written code, with its regulations, that was against us and that stood opposed to us; he took it away, nailing it to the cross.

COLOSSIANS 2:13–14

TEMPTATION'S POISON

The graceful collection of lantana, bird-of-paradise, and wisteria (the list goes on) on a local hospital's grounds looks deceptively innocent. Until you read the signs! Every plant in this "sinister garden" bears a warning: "Toxic, entire plant" or "Toxic, fruit and seeds."

The message is clear: Do Not Eat! And yet the guide tells guests, "An alarming number scoff at warnings, saying that everything here is natural, therefore harmless. Natural, yes, but it's possible to die a 'natural death' by sampling!"

I gasped. "Surely nobody would dare," I whispered to my friend Millie as we shepherded the children back to school after a study trip. Millie looked at me darkly. "I'd have said the same about Adam and Eve," she replied.

Well, I might as well face it. I had given voice to what I wanted to believe. A berry to garnish the gossip . . . A leaf of criticism . . . A seed of self-pity. . .

Maybe I learned more than the children that day. We don't sin a little and get by with it, do we? It poisons us. And it harms others as well. I guess claiming that it is "natural" is the greatest evil of all. Only with God's help can we avoid that "sinister garden."

Choose the good and live.

JUNE MASTERS BACHER

Those who know your name will trust in you, for you, LORD, have never forsaken those who seek you.

PSALM 9:10

Those who trust in the LORD are like Mount Zion, which cannot be shaken but endures forever.

PSALM 125:1

Trust in the LORD forever, for the LORD, the LORD, is the Rock eternal.

ISAIAH 26:4

The LORD longs to be gracious to you; he rises to show you compassion. For the LORD is a God of justice. Blessed are all who wait for him!

ISAIAH 30:18

Blessed is he whose help is the God of Jacob, whose hope is in the LORD his God.

PSALM 146:5

Trust in the LORD and do good; dwell in the land and enjoy safe pasture.

PSALM 37:3

Whoever gives heed to instruction prospers, and blessed is he who trusts in the LORD.

PROVERBS 16:20

Blessed is the man who trusts in the LORD, whose confidence is in him. He will be like a tree planted by the water that sends out its roots by the stream. It does not fear when heat comes; its leaves are always green. It has no worries in a year of drought and never fails to bear fruit.

JEREMIAH 17:7–8

Nebuchadnezzar said, "Praise be to the God of Shadrach, Meshach and Abednego, who has sent his angel and rescued his servants! They trusted in him and defied the king's command and were willing to give up their lives rather than serve or worship any god except their own God."

DANIEL 3:28

He who trusts in the LORD will prosper.

PROVERBS 28:25

Anyone who trusts in him will never be put to shame.

ROMANS 10:11

Fear of man will prove to be a snare, but whoever trusts in the LORD is kept safe.

PROVERBS 29:25

When you pass through the waters, I will be with you; and when you pass through the rivers, they will not sweep over you. When you walk through the fire, you will not be burned; the flames will not set you ablaze.

ISAIAH 43:2

Trust in the LORD with all your heart and lean not on your own understanding.

PROVERBS 3:5

Blessed is the [one] who makes the LORD his trust, who does not look to the proud, to those who turn aside to false gods.

PSALM 40:4

The LORD is good, a refuge in times of trouble. He cares for those who trust in him.

NAHUM 1:7

FREEDOM TO TRUST

Trust is such a lovely word in a world thoroughly self-indulged and complicated. It is quiet. Simple. It represents freedom. Rest. Letting go.

A friend of ours, who had been down the battered road of infertility, longed for another baby. A perfect situation came about. A young birth mother who felt the only answer for her baby was adoption.

A precious baby girl was born. The adoptive couple came from another city to meet the birth mother and to take their new baby home. The birth mother signed the papers, releasing the baby from the hospital. But in the courtroom, days later, she broke down. She just couldn't give up her baby.

The couple's celebration turned to heartbreak. Immediately, they began to trust. Not to figure it all out, or judge the birth mother. They waited quietly. In a year, twin girls were born and theirs was the chosen family. They lost one, and God gave them back two.

There are very many unknowns in life. A husband's job. Our children's struggles. A tentative move. Critical talk behind our backs. A search for our own identity. Bills to pay. Aged parents to look after.

Let go completely. Trust. Live with it all in an open hand before God. Jesus promises he WILL work it all out.

ANN KIEMEL ANDERSON

The fear of the Lord—that is wisdom, and to shun evil is understanding.

JOB 28:28

I will instruct you and teach you in the way you
   should go;
   I will counsel you and watch over you.

PSALM 32:8

"I guide you in the way of wisdom and lead you along straight paths. When you walk, your steps will not be hampered; when you run, you will not stumble," says the LORD.

PROVERBS 4:11–12

Get wisdom, get understanding. . . . Do not forsake wisdom, and she will protect you; love her, and she will watch over you. Wisdom is supreme; therefore get wisdom. Though it cost all you have, get understanding.

PROVERBS 4:5–7

Whether you turn to the right or to the left, your ears will hear a voice behind you, saying, "This is the way; walk in it."

ISAIAH 30:21

The wisdom that comes from heaven is first of all pure; then peace-loving, considerate, submissive, full of mercy and good fruit, impartial and sincere.

JAMES 3:17

If you accept my words and store up my commands within you, turning your ear to wisdom and applying your heart to understanding, and if you call out for insight and cry aloud for understanding, and if you look for it as for silver and search for it as for hidden treasure, then you will understand the fear of the LORD and find the knowledge of God. For the LORD gives wisdom, and from his mouth come knowledge and understanding.

PROVERBS 2:1–6

Where then does wisdom come from? Where does understanding dwell? It is hidden from the eyes of every living thing, concealed even from the birds of the air. . . . God understands the way to it and he alone knows where it dwells.

JOB 28:20–21,23

The foolishness of God is wiser than man's wisdom, and the weakness of God is stronger than man's strength.

1 CORINTHIANS 1:25

Pay attention to my wisdom, listen well to my words of insight, that you may maintain discretion and your lips may preserve knowledge.

PROVERBS 5:1–2

Whoever listens to me will live in safety and be at ease, without fear of harm.

PROVERBS 1:33

If any of you lacks wisdom, he should ask God, who gives generously to all without finding fault, and it will be given to him.

JAMES 1:5

Teach us to number our days aright,
    that we may gain a heart of wisdom.

PSALM 90:12

The fear of the LORD is the beginning of wisdom;
    all who follow his precepts have good
        understanding.
To him belongs eternal praise.

PSALM 111:10

[Wisdom] cannot be bought with the finest gold, nor can its price be weighed in silver.

JOB 28: 15

WISDOM

INCREASING IN WISDOM

Wisdom comes when we examine the experiences God gives us and discern what we have (or should have) learned from them. Nothing that has happened to us should be wasted (Romans 8:28). Because it is sometimes painful, often we do not take the time or effort to discover the reason for the "gift" of our personal experiences. When we do not learn as we should, we stop growing until we learn those same lessons through another experience tailor-made by God to make us mature (James 1:2-4). Most often we gain insight into our experiences only after earnest, persistent prayer. Psalm 43 is a wonderful model of persistent prayer; it opens up to us a person searching to know what God wants to reveal about a specific experience.

Perhaps we should try writing out what we have learned about God, ourselves and life during and then after an important experience. As we learn these lessons, I think we'll find that we will not need to learn them again in exactly the same way! This increases our individual capacity to learn greater lessons and gain deeper wisdom (Matthew 13:12).

ROSEMARY JENSEN

A word aptly spoken is like apples of gold in settings of silver.

PROVERBS 25:11

How good is a timely word!

PROVERBS 15:23

The Sovereign LORD has given me an instructed tongue, to know the word that sustains the weary. He wakens me morning by morning, wakens my ear to listen like one being taught.

ISAIAH 50:4

Out of the overflow of the heart the mouth speaks.

MATTHEW 12:34

There should not be obscenity, foolish talk or coarse joking, which are out of place, but rather thanksgiving.

EPHESIANS 5:4

Let your conversation be always full of grace, seasoned with salt, so that you may know how to answer everyone.

COLOSSIANS 4:6

Do not let any unwholesome talk come out of your mouths, but only what is helpful for building others up according to their needs, that it may benefit those who listen.

EPHESIANS 4:29

An honest answer is like a kiss on the lips.

PROVERBS 24:26

Do everything without complaining or arguing.

PHILIPPIANS 2:14

Keep your tongue from evil and your lips from speaking lies. Turn from evil and do good; seek peace and pursue it.

PSALM 34:13–14

He who guards his lips guards his life, but he who speaks rashly will come to ruin.

PROVERBS 13:3

If anyone considers himself religious and yet does not keep a tight rein on his tongue, he deceives himself and his religion is worthless.

JAMES 1:26

Whoever would love life and see good days must keep his tongue from evil and his lips from deceitful speech.

1 PETER 3:10

The tongue of the righteous is choice silver, but the heart of the wicked is of little value.

PROVERBS 10:20

Speaking the truth in love, we will in all things grow up into him who is the Head, that is, Christ.

EPHESIANS 4:15

Reckless words pierce like a sword, but the tongue of the wise brings healing.

PROVERBS 12:18

The mouth of the righteous man utters wisdom, and his tongue speaks what is just.

PSALM 37:30

May my lips overflow with praise,
    for you teach me your decrees.
May my tongue sing of your word,
    for all your commands are righteous.

PSALM 119:171–172

God's Words of Life on

WORDS

A gossip betrays a confidence.

PROVERBS 11:13

Better a dry crust with peace and quiet than a house full of feasting, with strife.

PROVERBS 17:1

Truthful lips endure forever, but a lying tongue lasts only a moment.

PROVERBS 12:19

Without wood a fire goes out; without gossip a quarrel dies down.

PROVERBS 26:20

May the words of my mouth
    and the meditation of my heart
be pleasing in your sight, O LORD,
    my Rock and my Redeemer.

PSALM 19:14

Avoid godless chatter, because those who indulge in it will become more and more ungodly.

2 TIMOTHY 2:16

Set a guard over my mouth, O LORD;
    keep watch over the door of my lips.

PSALM 141:3

193

Let us not love with words or tongue but with actions and in truth.

1 JOHN 3:18

With the tongue we praise our Lord and Father, and with it we curse men, who have been made in God's likeness. Out of the same mouth come praise and cursing. This should not be. Can both fresh water and salt water flow from the same spring? My brothers, can a fig tree bear olives, or a grapevine bear figs? Neither can a salt spring produce fresh water.

JAMES 3:9–12

A PROBLEM OF THE MIND AND TONGUE

One of my young sons was trudging slowly up the stairs. When he reached the top, I asked him what was wrong.

"Oh, I was just praying." Quite curious now, I asked what he was praying about.

"I can't tell you," he insisted, "because if I do, you'll be mad." After much persuasion I convinced him that he could confide in me. So he explained that he was praying about a problem he had with his mind.

"A problem with your mind?" I asked, now more curious than ever, wondering what kind of problem a child of six could have with his mind.

"Well," he said, "You see, every time I pass by the living room, (where his sister was taking a lesson) I see my piano teacher, and my tongue sticks out."

Needless to say, it was hard to keep a straight face, but I took his problem seriously and assured him that God could, indeed, help him with it.

Later, on my knees beside the bathtub as I bathed this little fellow, I thought how I still struggle with the problem of controlling my mind and my tongue. I bowed my head, and asked the Lord to forgive me and to give me the mind and heart and attitude of Christ.

GIGI GRAHAM TCHIVIDJIAN

Diligent hands bring wealth.

PROVERBS 10:4

For six days, work is to be done, but the seventh day shall be your holy day, a Sabbath of rest to the LORD.

EXODUS 35:2

Six days you shall labor and do all your work, but the seventh day is a Sabbath to the LORD your God. On it you shall not do any work, neither you, nor your son or daughter, nor your manservant or maidservant, nor your ox, your donkey or any of your animals, nor the alien within your gates, so that your manservant and maidservant may rest, as you do.

DEUTERONOMY 5:13–14

The sluggard craves and gets nothing, but the desires of the diligent are fully satisfied.

PROVERBS 13:4

Sow your seed in the morning, and at evening let not your hands be idle, for you do not know which will succeed, whether this or that, or whether both will do equally well.

ECCLESIASTES 11:6

Make it your ambition to lead a quiet life, to mind your own business and to work with your hands, just as we told you, so that your daily life may win the respect of outsiders and so that you will not be dependent on anybody.

1 THESSALONIANS 4:11–12

Dishonest money dwindles away, but he who gathers money little by little makes it grow.

PROVERBS 13:11

All hard work brings a profit, but mere talk leads only to poverty.

PROVERBS 14:23

Do not take advantage of a hired man who is poor and needy, whether he is a brother Israelite or an alien living in one of your towns. Pay him his wages each day before sunset, because he is poor and is counting on it.

DEUTERONOMY 24:14–15

The laborer's appetite works for him; his hunger drives him on.

PROVERBS 16:26

A wife of noble character who can find?
  She is worth far more than rubies.
Her husband has full confidence in her
  and lacks nothing of value.
She brings him good, not harm,
  all the days of her life.
She selects wool and flax
  and works with eager hands.
She is like the merchant ships,
  bringing her food from afar.
She gets up while it is still dark;
  she provides food for her family
  and portions for her servant girls.
She considers a field and buys it;
  out of her earnings she plants a vineyard.
She sets about her work vigorously;
  her arms are strong for her tasks.
She sees that her trading is profitable,
  and her lamp does not go out at night.
In her hand she holds the distaff
  and grasps the spindle with her fingers.
She opens her arms to the poor
  and extends her hands to the needy.
When it snows, she has no fear for her household;
  for all of them are clothed in scarlet.
She makes coverings for her bed;
  she is clothed in fine linen and purple.
Her husband is respected at the city gate,

where he takes his seat among the elders of
    the land.
She makes linen garments and sells them,
    and supplies the merchants with sashes.
She is clothed with strength and dignity;
    she can laugh at the days to come.
She speaks with wisdom,
    and faithful instruction is on her tongue.
She watches over the affairs of her household
    and does not eat the bread of idleness.
Her children arise and call her blessed;
    her husband also, and he praises her:
"Many women do noble things,
 but you surpass them all."

PROVERBS 31:10–29

I know, O LORD, that a man's life is not his own; it
is not for man to direct his steps.

JEREMIAH 10:23

Do not love sleep or you will grow poor; stay
awake and you will have food to spare.

PROVERBS 20:13

The plans of the diligent lead to profit as surely as
haste leads to poverty.

PROVERBS 21:5

My heart took delight in all my work, and this was the reward for all my labor.

ECCLESIASTES 2:10

Jesus said, "Well done, good and faithful servant! You have been faithful with a few things; I will put you in charge of many things. Come and share your master's happiness!"

MATTHEW 25:21

God is not unjust; he will not forget your work and the love you have shown him as you have helped his people and continue to help them.

HEBREWS 6:10

Now we ask you . . . to respect those who work hard among you, who are over you in the Lord and who admonish you. Hold them in the highest regard in love because of their work.

1 THESSALONIANS 5:12–13

CAREER PLANS

I had an increasing feeling that I should be doing something new. Each day I seemed to grow more and more restless, wondering what in the world I wanted to do. Finally, my husband asked me if I had asked God what I should do.

I began to seek the Lord with all my heart, asking him what he had in mind for my life. I found peace quickly as I sought the Lord's plan for my life. Instead of asking for a special job, I asked the Lord to place me where I would fit in and where I was needed.

I have just finished my fourth year in a public secondary school. My job brings me fulfillment. There is no doubt that I am where I belong and doing what he would have me do. I pray for my one hundred teenagers daily, and I pray for grace to model a loving and caring attitude. I appreciate sometimes even being able to share a little of my faith. I occasionally tell my students how I appreciate their position in life, as I'm not sure of what I want to be when I grow up either. Right now the only career goal I have is to be living the plans God has for me, to be seeking him with all my heart. Are you?

SUE RICHARDS

Cast your cares on the Lord
and he will sustain you;
he will never let the righteous fall.

PSALM 55:22

Commit your way to the LORD;
trust in him and he will do this:
He will make your righteousness shine like the dawn,
the justice of your cause like the noonday sun.

PSALM 37:5–6

Commit to the LORD whatever you do, and your plans will succeed.

PROVERBS 16:3

Do not be anxious about anything, but in everything, by prayer and petition, with thanksgiving, present your requests to God. And the peace of God, which transcends all understanding, will guard your hearts and your minds in Christ Jesus.

PHILIPPIANS 4:6–7

Keep your lives free from the love of money and be content with what you have, because God has said, "Never will I leave you; never will I forsake you."

HEBREWS 13:5

WORRY

Look at the birds of the air; they do not sow or reap or store away in barns, and yet your heavenly Father feeds them. Are you not much more valuable than they? . . . Who of you by worrying can add a single hour to his life? And why do you worry about clothes? See how the lilies of the field grow. They do not labor or spin. Yet I tell you that not even Solomon in all his splendor was dressed like one of these. If that is how God clothes the grass of the field, which is here today and tomorrow is thrown into the fire, will he not much more clothe you, O you of little faith?

MATTHEW 6:26–30

Cast all your anxiety on God because he cares for you.

1 PETER 5:7

Jesus said, "I tell you, do not worry about your life, what you will eat; or about your body, what you will wear. Life is more than food, and the body more than clothes."

LUKE 12:22–23

Do not worry about tomorrow, for tomorrow will worry about itself. Each day has enough trouble of its own.

MATTHEW 6:34

Do not be afraid, little flock, for your Father has been pleased to give you the kingdom.

LUKE 12:32

The LORD himself goes before you and will be with you; he will never leave you nor forsake you. Do not be afraid; do not be discouraged.

DEUTERONOMY 31:8

"No one will be able to stand up against you all the days of your life. As I was with Moses, so I will be with you; I will never leave you nor forsake you," says the LORD.

JOSHUA 1:5

He who fears the LORD has a secure fortress.

PROVERBS 14:26

Have I not commanded you? Be strong and courageous. Do not be terrified; do not be discouraged, for the LORD your God will be with you wherever you go.

JOSHUA 1:9

We say with confidence, "The LORD is my helper; I will not be afraid. What can man do to me?"

HEBREWS 13:6

✿❧ ————————————————————————

The LORD gives strength to his people; the LORD blesses his people with peace.

PSALM 29:11

When you lie down, you will not be afraid; when you lie down, your sleep will be sweet.

PROVERBS 3:24

My flesh and my heart may fail, but God is the strength of my heart and my portion forever.

PSALM 73:26

Those who trust in the LORD are like Mount Zion, which cannot be shaken but endures forever.

PSALM 125:1

God did not give us a spirit of timidity, but a spirit of power, of love and of self-discipline.

2 TIMOTHY 1:7

"Don't be afraid," the prophet answered. "Those who are with us are more than those who are with them."

2 KINGS 6:16

The LORD is with you when you are with him. If you seek him, he will be found by you.

2 CHRONICLES 15:2

It is God who makes . . . us stand firm in Christ. He anointed us, set his seal of ownership on us, and put his Spirit in our hearts as a deposit, guaranteeing what is to come.

2 CORINTHIANS 1:21–22

But blessed is the man who trusts in the LORD, whose confidence is in him. He will be like a tree planted by the water that sends out its roots by the stream. It does not fear when heat comes; its leaves are always green. It has no worries in a year of drought and never fails to bear fruit.

JEREMIAH 17:7–8

Great peace have they who love your law,
    and nothing can make them stumble.

PSALM 119:165

In the day of my trouble I will call to you,
    for you will answer me.

PSALM 86:7

WORLD

Taking and Leaving
Your Burdens

I knew a Christian lady who had a very heavy tem-
poral burden . . . One day, when it seemed especially heavy, she noticed lying on the table near her
a little tract. She picked it up and began to read it,
little knowing, however, that it was to create a revo-
lution in her whole experience.

The story was of a poor woman who had been car-
ried triumphantly through a life of unusual sorrow.
She was giving the history of her life to a kind visitor
on one occasion, and at the close the visitor said
feelingly, "I do not see how you could bear so much
sorrow!"

"I did not bear it," was the quick reply; "the Lord
bore it for me."

"Yes," said the visitor, "that is the right way. We must
take our troubles to the Lord." [The poor woman
replied,] "We must do more than that: we must leave
them there. Most people take their burdens to him,
but they bring them away with them again, and are
just as worried and unhappy as ever. But I take mine
and I leave them with him, and come away and forget them. I do this over and over, until at last I just
forget I have any worries."

HANNAH WHITALL SMITH

207

ACKNOWLEDGMENTS
EXCERPTS TAKEN FROM:

The African-American Devotional Bible: New International Version. Copyright © 1997 by The Zondervan Corporation. All rights reserved. Devotional thoughts by Reverend Dr. Cheryl Clemetson, Reverend Rosalyn Grant Frederick, Reverend Dr. Delores Carpenter, and Reverend Dr. Alicia D. Byrd.

Diamonds in the Dust by Joni Eareckson Tada. Copyright ©1993 by Joni Eareckson Tada. (Grand Rapids, MI: Zondervan Publishing House, 1993). All rights reserved.

Meditation Moments by Millie Stamm. Formerly published as *Meditation Moments for Women.* Copyright © 1967 by Zondervan Publishing House. (Grand Rapids, MI: Zondervan Publishing House, 1967)All rights reserved.

A Rose by any Other Name Would Still Have Aphids by Mab Graff Hoover. Copyright © 1992 by Mab Graff Hoover. All rights reserved.

Seniors' Devotional Bible: New International Version. Copyright © 1995 by The Zondervan Corporation. All rights reserved. Devotional thoughts by Jill Briscoe, Kathryn Hillen, Carole Mayhall, Elisabeth Elliot, Hannah Whitall Smith, and Jean Shaw.

Women's Devotional Bible: New International Version. Copyright © 1990 by The Zondervan Corporation. All rights reserved. Devotional thoughts by Gien Karssen, Mary Jane Worden, Florence Littauer, Mab Graff Hoover, Jean E. Syswerda, Jeanette Lockerbie, Alma Barkman, Debbie Smith, Marjorie Holmes, June Masters Bacher, Gini Andrews, Sue Richards, Mrs. Charles E. Cowman, Rosemary Jensen, Karen Burton Mains, Rebecca Manley Pippert, Gigi Graham Tchividjian, Carol L. Baldwin, Doris Haase.